Punk Style

Subcultural Style Series

ISSN: 1955–0629

Series editor: Steve Redhead, Charles Sturt University

The *Subcultural Style* Series comprises short, accessible books that each focus on a specific subcultural group and their fashion. Each book in the series seeks to define a specific subculture and its quest to exist on the fringes of mainstream culture, which is most visibly expressed within a subculture's chosen fashions and styles. The books are written primarily for students of fashion and dress but will also be of interest to those studying cultural studies, sociology, and popular culture. Each title will draw upon a range of international examples and will be well illustrated. Titles in the series include: *Punk Style, Queer Style, Body Style* and *Fetish Style.*

Punk Style

Monica Sklar

B L O O M S B U R Y
LONDON · NEW DELHI · NEW YORK · SYDNEY

Bloomsbury Academic

An imprint of Bloomsbury Publishing Plc

50 Bedford Square	1385 Broadway
London	New York
WC1B 3DP	NY 10018
UK	USA

www.bloomsbury.com

Bloomsbury is a trade mark of Bloomsbury Publishing Plc

First published 2013

British Library Cataloguing-in-Publication Data
A catalogue record for this book is available from the British Library.

ISBN: HB: 978-1-8478-8423-7
PB: 978-1-8478-8422-0
ePub: 978-0-8578-5305-9

Library of Congress Cataloging-in-Publication Data
A catalog record for this book is available from the Library of Congress.

Typeset by Apex CoVantage, LLC, Madison, WI, USA
Printed and bound in India

**For Harlo, Levi,
and my parents**

Contents

List of Illustrations

Acknowledgments

I would like to thank the following people for their contribution to this effort, for providing me this significant chance to explore and disseminate my research passions, and for working closely with me on the development of this project: Bloomsbury editors Julia, Anna, Emily, and Hannah; and series editor Steve Redhead.

Thank you also to Theresa Winge for introducing me to this opportunity and believing in me and mentoring me early on in the process; to Lisa Santandrea for her painstaking editing and thoughtful contributions; and to all who participated in the portion of this project that came from my dissertation—including the five focus group participants, the more than 200 survey respondents, and especially the twenty invaluable interviewees without whom this research would have been so lacking. Sharing of those experiences provided the soul of this research.

Additionally, I would like to convey my gratitude to the interviewees from around the globe who participated solely for the book project, including Marco, Roger, Brian, Sara, Snooky, and Zandra, all of whom have been so generous with their time, memories, and insights; David Muggleton for his reading through the manuscript and enthusiastic support; Roger, Jon, Tanya, the Manic Panic team; Amanda, Grace, Sarah, Kime, Julie, Kimberly, Alec, Jen, and all of the "models" who provided images for this book, whether they were included or not. I appreciate your windows into punk style; also Chad Rieder for assisting with capturing our personal collection.

My appreciation also goes to Dana Raidt for the priceless in-the-know transcription of the interviews; and to all of the instructors, colleagues, and professional friends who have supported me through lessons, collaboration, and inspiration, as well as commented on or edited this work, which in part consolidated years of research projects through many graduate-level courses. Thank you particularly to Dr. Marilyn DeLong for her thoughtful advising, mentoring, committee work, endless edits of my dissertation manuscript, and my inclusion on her other research projects, which helped shape my understanding of how to research. I also want to acknowledge my dissertation committee of Drs. Joanne B. Eicher, Kim K. Johnson, and Jim Bequette, for their varied perspectives on the study of dress, culture, and history, and many edits to manuscripts. Furthermore, my anthropology class led by Dr. Mark Pedelty worked through Chapter 1 and helped frame the book as it transitioned from schoolwork to a manuscript. Thank you also to Quinton for an early read and tips of process.

A grateful nod to all of the friends and members of the subcultural and particularly punk and hardcore scenes I've been a part of, particularly the metro Detroit community, but also those friends I have made internationally. We are family. You continue to inspire me.

Longtime friends have been so supportive; many have been in my life since childhood and are my sisters. I thank you for your unwavering friendship even as we have flown in so many directions; we always fly back to each other.

Everyone I have worked with at Worn Through provided kinship, collaboration, inspirations, and support of my research as a student, independent scholar, and otherwise busy person! May we continue to develop projects together.

I would also like to acknowledge my extended Rosenberg family for its passion for learning and education that has driven me to pursue my goals; the support and loyalty from my in-law family and all other extended family through the years; my brother Jeff and his family for ongoing encouragement; and of course my parents, Kathy and Gary Sklar, for their endless endorsement of my studies and of my various life pursuits, no matter my hair color, as well as their utmost emphasis on and respect for education in the classroom and through all of life.

Most of all, I want to acknowledge Harlo for his true partnership in all things, his immeasurable amount of time and effort assisting with all of my academic research endeavors, and his vast understanding of not only subculture but seemingly everything else, including me; finally, my thanks to Levi for keeping things interesting and providing something even better to do on a weekend night than any show.

–1–

Introduction

I entered high school in the fall of 1991, a year often referred to as "the year punk broke" (Spitz 2011).[1] This was a point in society when the dam burst and the counterculture came rushing into mainstream interest. The boundaries defining culture and subculture became completely blurred. Music, fashion, and personalities from the punk underground became very much part of the mainstream cultural milieu. While punk's lineage predates 1991 by over fifteen years—and it had seen crossover success before—it had never succeeded to the level it was to reach in this era. By the 1990s, punk had surpassed its infancy and developed into a robust subculture. It had also begun to battle with unprecedented mainstream acceptance. Much of my adolescence and the identity I developed as an adult were shaped by this conflicted era when punk and the mainstream wove in and out of cohesion. One of the areas that struck the loudest chord for me was punk style. Its aggressive presentation—a mix of artful whimsy, "couldn't care less" attitude, and carefully placed "in the know" symbolism—drew me in.

Spring forward to today. Punk style has continued to evolve and spawn new life in the Internet era. The Web has forced punk to once again reevaluate its place in the world. New issues have sprung up that challenge punk's original do-it-yourself (DIY) and antiauthoritarian themes. These challenges include defining legitimacy and confronting the commonplace punk imagery that is pervasive today on corporate websites, blogs, YouTube, and social networking sites. Today punk style—a visual identity once so hard fought to create—can be purchased with a quick click of a mouse. Does the countercultural identity imbued in this attire also arrive in the bubble-wrapped package on one's doorstep? This is a contemporary challenge to the integrity of punk style. On the other hand, social networking and enthusiasts' blogs also connect subcultural souls who would otherwise never meet, and help to enlighten the masses about the powerful messages the symbols of punk were attempting to communicate.

Between "the year punk broke" and the Internet era, I embarked on an academic study of dress, design, and visual culture. During this time I watched and analyzed punk's continued development through the lens of both a participant and an educated observer.

Subcultural Style Today

Subcultures have long played a significant role in the development of popular visual signifiers, which are often the catalyst for mainstream styles. Punk is one of the most influential and highly visible of modern subcultures, alongside other formerly underground scenes such as hip-hop, goth, and electronic dance music. Many elements of punk dress have become iconic in popular culture, and yet some of their implications have changed since the movement's origins in the mid-to-late 1970s. While punk style has simultaneously maintained some of its relevance and original subcultural intent, it has also developed mainstream appeal and cachet, although in an adulterated form.

Time spent at the Mall of America in Minnesota, where I currently live, has provided abundant insight for me as both an academic/social researcher and someone who identifies with the punk scene. The Mall of America is an epicenter of mainstream consumer culture, a product powerhouse for middle American consumer goods. Apparel and beauty items are generally priced at the low-to-mid range while some high-end luxury goods are available in its department stores.

Perhaps surprisingly then, the Mall of America has a vast selection of punk-influenced fashions on display and available for sale. The punk influence would be obvious to anyone aware of the subculture's iconography. However, to those who are not familiar with punk's colors, patterns, and band logos, the clothes could appear simply as appealing palettes in a fad. Generally, these fashions on sale reflect the style of early to mid-1980s punk, incorporating bright colors and graffiti paint. However, there are some references to 1970s punk styles, including studded belts and cut-and-paste letters and graphics. And, in a notably miraculous transition, some rather mundane garments have been transformed from staid to mildly subversive by the use of the skull and crossbones image.

These plentiful, punk-themed items seem to lack the spirit I have come to identify with and expect from punk style. It is difficult to analyze the symbolism of objects that are continually recycled and evolving in either their physical aesthetics or their community of wearers, particularly when much of the style itself originated with reappropriated looks. Perhaps the attire at the mall is still loaded with punk meaning. But this is unlikely. As 1970s and 1980s styles are revived through the cyclical nature of fashion, retooled as "retro," punk symbols may simply be considered vintage imagery to be appreciated at the surface level. Those who purchase these styles are less likely to be self-identified punks than young adults interested in the latest trends. Today, punk-influenced style is seen on twentysomethings packing rock clubs. It fills the racks at malls, is sold on the auction block, and is on display in museum exhibitions. Meanwhile, legions of self-identified punks across the globe continue to wear their own variations of punk style, dressing in garments and accessories imbued with subcultural cues, which have often been produced and then consumed through alternative methods. In the early twenty-first century, punk style is as relevant and curious as ever.

Introducing Punk Style

In the beginning, punk-styled apparel was self-made or pieced together through bricolage. It was available for purchase only through specific channels, which included small boutiques and fetish retailers, ads in fanzines, or punk events. Today, these formerly hard to find clothes are widely available through chain stores and websites. People can dabble in numerous subcultures through the Internet, networking with others from around the globe and learning about fashion trends, artistic styles, political movements, and musical directions. Contemporary involvement in the punk subculture does not require the investment of time or energy it did for previous generations. This inspires the question: Is dressing like a punk enough to *be* punk? Maybe. Maybe not.

Punk remains an esoteric and amorphous concept. Consequently, it is difficult to define and to categorize its components as punk or not punk. My research attempts to describe punk style and explain its history and motivations. I deliberately allowed interviewees and all media sourced for this analysis to self-identify as punk, rather than coming into the project with preconceived parameters. This oft misunderstood subculture began in the 1970s, in major metropolitan areas in the United Kingdom and the United States—a vital new way to perform subcultural ideas

Fig. 1.1 Pins and buttons representing symbols, brands, ideas, and bands associated with punk and subculture; one inch is the most common size (copyright Monica Sklar and Harlo Petoskey).

that incorporated its own art, music, dress, and lifestyles. From its 1970s origins through its various present-day incarnations, punk is commonly rooted in those who are in some way disenfranchised from society. Self-identified punks may be critical of mainstream art, politics, popular culture, consumerism, lifestyles, or sexual and social mores. Punk dress was rooted in a desire to be ironic and anti-hegemonic; it reinvented mainstream styles to critique society via bricolage and appropriation (Baron 1989; Hebdige 1979; Polhemus 1994; Rombes 2005; Szatmary 1996). Many elements of punk dress, such as combat boots, studded belts, and vibrantly dyed hair, have become iconic and stable in popular culture, yet symbolism and meanings have changed throughout time (Bennett 2006).

Popular perception, at least in academic critiques, presumes that punk is rooted in the music. But, in fact, the music and fashion have always developed simultaneously and in conjunction (which is true of many subcultures beyond punk). The early days of the punk scene were a blend of fashion, music, politics, hooliganism, youth culture, avant-garde artists, intellectuals, societal outcasts, and the generally disenfranchised. Punk today continues to contain most of those elements, and thus it is not solely a musical form, or even a music-based community. Instead, it is a lifestyle choice often shaped into communities by individuals who think along the same lines. Music is an outlet for the expression of ideas and creativity, and punk music shows are a gathering place for the community. "I tend to view punk as much less about a style of clothing and more so about a way of being in the world," said Matt, a self-identified punk.

Not all of those who self-identify as punk share the same perspective on subcultural dress. Opinions about punk and punk style can vary widely depending on levels of personal commitment, the time period when one discovered and embraced punk, and distinct individual experiences (Fox 1987; Traber 2008; Wood 2003). Punk dress can function on many levels within and outside the punk community. Therefore this style is a postmodern example of aesthetics within a cultural movement that can be simultaneously subversive and acceptable, depending on context, viewer, wearer, and intent (Efland, Freedman, and Stuhr 1996; Henderson and DeLong 2000; Sturken and Cartwright 2001).

Some individuals lean toward punk styles as a fanciful expression of self or in an attempt to buck contemporary trends. For others, punk dress represents one facet of larger counter-hegemonic agendas played out in other aspects of their lives. As such, the styles can mark inclusion in a tribe (Bennett 1999; Polhemus 1996) and the benefits of that kinship. For many, the body serves as a site of political representation and is used to make a strong statement regarding standards of beauty, gender, sexuality, social mores, and consumer values. All of these reasons act as motivators for dressing in punk style, but can also build the basis for choosing almost any form of dress. Therefore, diving further into why some choose punk style is a worthwhile pursuit. This postmodern slant to a supposed cohesive group is a point of confusion. Although outsiders perceive punk as a unified subculture— and indeed there are many communal aspects, including iconic forms of dress—it is actually a broad-based movement that allows for deeply personal interpretations. Thus, participants will have varied definitions of and explanations for their dress behaviors.

Additionally, the punk subculture has developed in numerous ways over its four decades of existence. Progress in technology and globalization have contributed to the expansion of music, and there is more accessibility for anyone to participate in youth and anti-hegemonic subcultures. Previously, an individual had to demonstrate a strong commitment to be involved in subcultures such as punk. Growing a community and knowledge building took place only at in-person events such as bands' shows, which could be hours or even time zones away. Thus, it was not uncommon for people to invest energy in only one subculture. Furthermore, even within a subculture, participants form splinter groups with other individuals who share their specific interests and desired aesthetic. The larger subculture and the subgroups within are in a continuous and dynamic process of evolution.

The Iconic Punk Style: Truth and Fiction

Certain characteristics of punk dress have come to signify punk, particularly in the mainstream media and when nearly anyone is making a quick reference. That is the image of a sneering youth wearing something akin to a leather motorcycle jacket, tattered black band logo T-shirt skinny-fitting bondage pants or ripped jeans, combat boots, studded or safety pin metal accessories, and vibrant body modifications such as heavy cosmetics and/or a colored mohawk. These signifiers are rooted in fashion designs, subcultural trends, and popular street styles that have been incorporated into punk dress since the 1970s. However, they may not tell a complete story of punk style.

Interestingly, multiple self-identified punks interviewed for this research started their response to the question "how would you describe punk dress *in general*" with the phrase "I guess" and other qualifiers and pauses, which could have indicated they were trying to put themselves in the shoes of someone else looking in on the punk scene; they were trying to describe what an outsider might see. When asked to generalize, they likely signified conflict in doing so by including in their responses "I guess" or "might." While their answers did support the idea that punk has an iconic look, they also reflected the understanding that this look is often merely a caricature, presenting only a narrow viewpoint. The interviewees' tepid answers were in opposition to the confidence and lack of qualifiers in their responses to the question "describe punk dress as you personally have worn it" and other related inquiries into their own punk styling.

> *I guess* I still think of it as the classic '80s punk. You know, liberty spikes and colored hair and piercings and tattoos and leather jackets. And for girls, little plaid miniskirts and ripped hose and combat boots.—Tara

Someone might say liberty spikes, denim jackets, with spikes on it, pyramid spikes, and Sid Vicious,[2] like a padlock around your neck, ripped-up jeans, whatever. Twelve-hole Doc Martens … you know safety pins, but I think that sort of represents London in '77[3] more so than it represents all of punk.—Augie

The picture they paint is both reality and stereotype. Many self-identified punks look exactly as described. But, upon further investigation, it is clear that the image of the mohawked, tartan-wearing, spikes and chains adorned, middle-finger-waving punk is not wholly accurate as a descriptor of all who identify as punk. Some of those interviewed for this book do, in fact, dress close to that iconic style as a form of artistic and identity expression. It is not that the look is fabrication or has ceased to exist; it is simply not as rigid a punk norm as outsiders may believe.

The iconic punk style, mostly rooted in 1970s British fashion, is still in existence, but it has developed into a form of caricature and few choose to utilize all of its most exaggerated elements simultaneously. This is particularly true among those punks who are not in a performance context (i.e., not on stage in a band). It certainly has lived on throughout the decades and been transformed to meet the expressive needs of punks around the globe, but its origins and the apex of its popularity were specific to a time and place—since then, other looks have represented other punk genres, times, and contexts.

Punk style always had leaders and followers. As with any genre of dress, the followers were inspired by and often mimicked the leaders' styles of dress. Also, societal issues that simultaneously affect many people could result in a shared motivation to dress in a certain manner. Examples might include a conflict such as war, a financial change such as depression, or a concern such as climate change. Yet individuality was always an important component of punk style. Furthermore, the nature of garments that are ripped, reconstructed, and repurposed means there are limits to how exactly they can be reproduced—thus the style lends itself to uniqueness. Consequently, there is both cohesiveness and uniqueness in punk style.

One thing to consider is that there were always other kinds of punk dress besides "the iconic look", such as the 1970s New York look rooted in jeans, T-shirts, and tattered American street wear mixed with a few avant-garde elements. This look remains popular and influential, especially within the United States. Another consideration is that many subsequent movements within punk or adjacent to punk have influenced punk style or have been incorporated into the overall aesthetic. This is especially true of later generations of punks, such as mods and glams, who appropriated the stylistic influences of previous generations. Hence, today multiple modes of appearance would qualify as punk style. For example, contemporary punks sometimes dress in more subtle ways. Audra said: "I don't have an excessive amount of plaid clothing or leather pants with zippers or any high heel boots." Matt added: "I never had a real weird haircut or anything like that. And never really owned a leather jacket that I considered to fit in as punk in any way."

This diversity is true going back to the first generation of punks in the 1970s. Members of the band The Damned dressed themselves from government surplus and costume supply stores while the infamous band the Sex Pistols dressed in statement fashions by designers Vivienne Westwood and Malcolm McLaren. It was important for each segment of the scene to have an individual style, thus overlapping ideas may have become iconic, but there was no consistent look (Gray 2004).

Part of the reason a narrow image, became popularized was to simplify an understanding of punk by those outside the scene. This was particularly useful to the media of the 1970s looking to explain this new theme that mesmerized and revolted them. Marco Pirroni, who was an active participant in the initial British punk scene as well as a member of the band Adam and the Ants, said:

> They started to investigate, not investigate. They sent a couple reporters down to the shop, basically … they got some pics with Steve Severin from [Siouxsie and the] Banshees, and put like "This is a punk. Punks wear safety pins. Punks wear torn clothes … Punks wear leather trousers." … This is the first time the rest of the country had ever seen a punk. So the thing I always think is funny … punk fashion really comes from the mainstream telling you what punk fashion is.

Subsequently, outsiders learned about punk primarily through the media, and the new converts had an aesthetic shaped by what was presented to them, thus creating a cyclical truth with the power to endure.

The challenge with creating a costume dubbed punk is that it does unify people to a set of ideas; however, it lacks some of the original intension of creativity, individuality, and antiauthority, including in how one dresses. The contemporary punk attempts to find a balance between obligation to that ideology and embracing personal core ideas. For some, looking 100 percent punk is a way to fully embrace the theme, while for others it is stepping into a costume of a time/place not as easily stereotyped as the image represents. Marco added: "They completely missed the point. These fashions were kind of evolving, breathing things made up of lots of people, you know, they weren't just a thing."

Background Literature

The discussion of punk is wide ranging. The literature included in the review for this research accepted texts that addressed punk and subculture from an array of viewpoints, and often they either defined terms or at least used the word *punk* as a root of the texts' material. Interviews were conducted with individuals who expressed an interest in and connection to the ideas of punk and to its related subcultures without my holding the interviewees to strict guidelines of a preconceived definition. Consequently, this research did not measure an individual's level of punkness, or that individual's or research text's interpretation of punk dress. I simply had to take proclamations of identification as punk and descriptions of punk dress as valid. However, common themes did emerge from the research to help examine an ambiguous style and gain insight, especially when dictionary definitions prove insufficient.

It was imperative to establish a foundation of what constitutes *dress* or *style* for this research. Mary Ellen Roach-Higgins and Joanne Eicher said the term *dress* "not only signifies the apparel worn by men and women but also refers to the act of covering the body with clothes and accessories" (1965: 1). Eicher uses a sociocultural perspective to define *dress* in more detail as:

> A system of nonverbal communication that enhances human beings' interaction as they move in space and time. As a coded sensory system, dressing the body occurs when human beings modify their bodies visually or through other sensory measures by manipulating color, texture, scent, sounds, and taste or by supplementing their bodies with articles of clothing and accessories, and jewelry. (2000: 422)

This definition is clear regarding the physical and communicative qualities of dress but is vague regarding attitudinal factors, context, and how the dress is embodied.

Marilyn DeLong and Mike Brake add depth regarding how dress is embodied. An aesthetic-oriented view of dress focuses on the *apparel body construct* (DeLong 1998). This is defined as "a visual form that results from the interaction of apparel on the human body; a concept of this physical object based on sensory data" (DeLong 1998: 339). The apparel body construct combines the styling with the body inhabiting it within its cultural context and incorporates ideas about value. Brake's description of *style* is commonly used in sociological literature, particularly contemporary studies of subculture. He brings together three primary elements: "A. 'Image,' appearance composed of costume, accessories such as a hair-style, jewelry, and artifacts. B. 'Demeanor,' made up of expression, gait, and posture. Roughly this is what the actors wear and how they wear it. C. 'Argot,' a special vocabulary and how it is delivered" (1985: 11–12). Brake's ideas take into account whether, for example, a punk can inhabit any dress artifact and make it "punk," or whether anyone can inhabit a "punk" artifact and then they are punk. Brake's "image," "demeanor," and "argot" also can be useful in dealing with issues of authenticity, which permeate discussions of punk.

An amalgamation of each of these outlooks on dress and style develops useful parameters to examine the appearances within the punk subculture. Therefore punk dress may include visual and material representations such as combat boots and tattoos and numerous other adaptations to the body that reflect a punk identity. It may also include embodiment, attitudinal and contextual factors that influence the use and interpretation of those bodily adaptations, as well as how successfully the wearer's meaning is communicated through the use of the dress objects. This can be witnessed in how natural or comfortable someone appears in his or her clothes. It is also reflected in garnering the intended reaction from viewers.

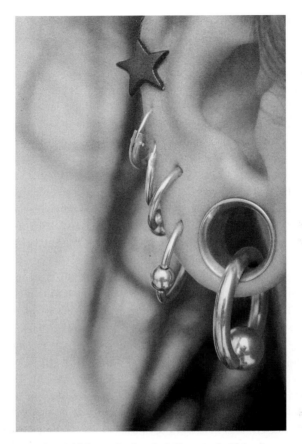

Fig. 1.2 Multiple ear piercings including stretched lobes (copyright Getty, photographer Medioimages/Photodisc, collection Photodisc).

Previous Research on Subculture and Dress

Punk is often overlooked in fashion literature when studying dress from a high fashion point of view or from the viewpoint of cultural or business analysis. While dress studies loosely predate the twentieth century, only in the past century has dress scholarship fully developed and grown into many branches in the academic system. Dress has been studied in many ways from its roots in agriculture, the home, and the family, to its relevance in industrialization and then business study, through its sociocultural implications, and finally to its artistic and aesthetic value. Literature regarding subcultural style is thin and the concepts are under investigated. This particular prominent subculture, with its forty-year history and influence on contemporary style, remains a bit elusive in terms of thorough analysis. A small handful of relevant analyses have received acclaim and given punk style recognition.

Dick Hebdige's 1979 book *Subculture: The Meaning of Style* is often regarded as the seminal text on the correlation between dress and subculture. Hebdige's book evaluated the relationship of subcultural movements, including punk, with their visual identities. He looked at the motivations, context, and background that created, facilitated, and perpetuated the signification of these style choices. The text is known for introducing racial and ethnic issues into the development of subcultures, a new concept of the time that shifted perceptions away from the previous positioning of subcultures as class-based reactionary movements (Evans 1997). Hebdige's *Subculture* is also known for its in-depth discussion about the connection of dress and subculture, not as simply a descriptive tool to move on to another subject, but as the primary variable discussed.

Prior to Hebdige's book, other texts did address the relationship between dress and subculture, yet not specifically punk, in part because some predated punk. In fact, *Subculture* is seen as fourth in a line of books that link style and countercultures together for review. These were all associated with the University of Birmingham Centre for Contemporary Cultural Studies (Muggleton 2002), commonly known as CCCS, whose theories and writings have traveled the arc from inventive, to highly esteemed, to a point of controversy and critique among subculture researchers. This latter position results from the limitations of this early work, which is now often seen as historically significant but possibly no longer accurate or relevant (Bennett 1999, 2006; Calluori 1985; Evans 1997; Muggleton 2002; Sweet 2005).

Before the CCCS, the beginnings of modern subcultural study could be found in the 1920s and 1930s, through the naturalistic research at the Chicago School. That led to the 1950s and 1960s behavioral and normative foci, which equated subculture with deviance and criminal behavior (Levine and Stumpf 1983). This work has resonated through the decades, as can be seen in the scrutiny of the black trench coats frequently worn by the infamous shooters at Columbine High School in 1999 (Ogle and Eckman 2002) and the 1994 wrongful murder conviction—not resolved until 2012—of teenagers known as the West Memphis Three, which was in large part based on their preference for black T-shirts and interest in heavy metal and the occult.

By the 1960s and 1970s, the common research angle was moving away from studying subcultures as negative and criminal reactionary groups. The new idea was that subcultures resulted from complex interactions between power groups. It was then, in the 1970s, that the CCCS produced such writings as Stuart Hall and Tony Jefferson's oft referenced 1976 book, *Resistance through Rituals: Youth Subcultures in Post War Britain*, and finally Hebdige's *Subculture* (Baron 1989; Bennett 1999).

Since Hebdige's seminal text, an array of publications have acknowledged the relationship of dress and subculture, some with more insight than others, in varied manners. It is clear that the impact of punk itself was culturally significant, and its aesthetics and attitude resonate through many facets of society. Thus, the topic of punk has received significant coverage in the popular press, in acclaimed and robust historical accounts of its history, such as *Please Kill Me: The Uncensored Oral*

History of Punk (McNeil and McCain 1996) and *England's Dreaming: Anarchy, Sex Pistols, Punk Rock, and Beyond* (Savage 1991). Valuable information has created a body of knowledge about the culture and its personalities, particularly its most recognized named members, but voids remain when it comes to an in-depth analysis specifically pertaining to punk dress style.

I performed a critical literature review of journal articles published from 1979 to 2007 that prominently focused on subculture and dress. The goal was to see if perhaps the depth was within the details of individual journal articles. The year 1979 was chosen as the starting point to determine what research had taken place since the publication of Hebdige's influential book. This review of articles revealed the dominant themes in the contemporary literature. One of the most striking findings was that punk was the most prominently featured subcultural group under analysis regarding dress and subculture, with others being hip-hop, goth, ravers, and skateboarders, among others. Commonly discussed were variations on punk, beginning with its origins in multiple major Western cities and countries, particularly England, where the CCCS was located, through its many incarnations in its four-decade lifespan. Punk was the topic in a relatively small number of studies overall, but in higher quantity than other subcultural groups studied, which is partly a testament to the high visibility, influence, and resiliency of the subculture. Yet again, with all of the focus on punk, even in the highly specific world of research studies and its corresponding journal articles, dress and punk were linked mostly as descriptive tools or secondary variables. I later updated my research to include journal articles from 2008 to 2012 as well as theses, within which there had been an uptick in research specifically linking punk and style, increasing the dialogue regarding issues of authenticity, performance, art movements, and power dynamics (Cherry and Mellins 2011; Force 2009; Patterson 2007; Schmitt 2011; Van Ham 2009). Upon finishing my journal article research, I speculated that perhaps the lack of published articles did not indicate a lack of research, but perhaps the research was moving in other directions for dissemination. I undertook a second critical literature review to investigate what is out there in the written form on punk and dress.

Few books were found directly connecting punk and dress in any manner. Commonly, those texts that were found were in anthologies, essay collections, and other edited texts, which contained only a limited piece. Punk dress is also featured in some books on subculture and style or body modification with punk placed within a larger context (Winge 2012). Other notable examples of formats to disseminate research on punk dress include museum exhibitions such as the Metropolitan Museum of Art's *Punk: From Chaos to Couture* and *AngloMania: Tradition and Transgression in British Fashion,* auction preparations such as those of Christie's and Sotheby's, and the display or discussion of personal and institutional collections such as the Contemporary Wardrobe in London. The publications and press surrounding these can be quite stimulating and informative, yet they are generally edited texts, introductions to catalogs, or media interviews with the associated professionals, thus limiting the scope possible in explanation or theory addressing the wider history and significance of punk dress, as well as often eliminating an insider angle as the garments are frequently not discussed by wearers. They also often focus on the specific materials in the exhibitions or collections, so lack breadth. Similarly, there is an array of stellar representations of punk dress from photo retrospectives of photographers such as Jim Jocoy chronicling early Los Angeles, Roberta Bayley capturing early New York, Glen E. Friedman memorializing the emerging hybrid between punk, skateboarding, and hip-hop in the 1980s, and Chrissy Piper capturing the underground 1990s hardcore scene throughout the United States. These books tend to highlight some other aspect of punk, such as music, geography, or a time period, but style features proximately because of the visually driven medium. Some of the photographic collections did include scholarly introductions or other passages with historic insight from insiders, yet they too are restricted in their analysis on the dress with that not being the primary concern of those volumes.

This lack of thorough research linking punk and dress is even more glaring in light of the large quantity of books and online publications regarding punk aligning it to other forms of design. There were design-oriented books in text and nontext formats connecting punk to interiors, typography and graphic design, fine art, and cinema, among other mediums. The closest in this arena to the goals of my search would probably be the books produced by and for the modern craft movement, which contains a large number of people who consider themselves part of the punk movement and who use their punk ideologies and aesthetics in their crafting. These books are frequently of a "how-to" nature; however, they are about dress and do commonly contain introductions, commentary, and some level of discussion as to the motivations and purpose for constructing the craft from modern and punk standpoints.

In addition to the books linking punk with design methods other than dress, there are also a significant number of texts aligning punk with many facets of life and culture. These include various analyses of how punk culture relates to topics such as parenthood and family life, gender identity and relationships, and health, fitness, and nutrition. Finally, there are even a handful of marketing, retailing, and business books regarding punk. The volume of varied literature on punk, including that in conjunction with design, leaves a disturbing void regarding punk and dress, in particular when dress is one of the most iconic ways punk is considered. It is of note that some of those texts touch on punk dress in limited ways, but none use the two concepts as the primary ideas of emphasis.

It was found that researchers have used methods other than the printed word to distribute projects into the overall body of knowledge. There have been a handful of oral presentations on punk dress given at conferences from organizations such as the Costume Society of America, the International Apparel and Textile Association, and the Popular Culture Association. There have also been oral presentations featuring punk dress given at conferences in fields such as American culture, women's studies, and sociology. It is possible some of the conference material will be published at a later date.

Documentary films and reality TV comprise other routes researchers are taking to present their material on punk style. As with the other mediums, these representations generally have another focus, such as a tattoo shop's employees (reality TV) or the Afro-punk movement in general (in which dress and body image are discussed). Notable exceptions are the BBC miniseries *British Style Genius* (2009) and *Punk Britannia* (2012) that featured brief but thoughtful segments of well-researched analysis of punk dress.

Websites, blogs, and other Internet resources also report information on punk style, sometimes quite academically and thoroughly. Often these sources provide some of the most carefully crafted presentations, frequently from historians, collectors, punk community insiders, and apparel designers; examples include *The Look*, *Threadbared*, and *Worn Through* (author's blog). The nature of the Web leads to the inclusion of infinite voices and to fewer limits on editing, page space, and even a lax attitude toward image rights, which can make for fabulous reading and viewing for the reader; however, this is a fluid mechanism for distributing information and individual posts or blogs may not stay available live on the Web, or may be buried deep within the archives of a frequently posting blog, and thus may not be referenced and viewed with ease and permanence.

Finally, tidbits and pieces spring up in TV shows, and while there is an array of other materials through various popular press media on punk dress, commonly they are not scholarly or educational but primarily serve entertainment purposes or occasionally fashion-oriented trend news. All of this demonstrates there is a great deal of interest in touching on the area of punk style, yet there has been limited output focused on it.

The Literature: Punk's Time to Get Attention in Fashion Research

Although punk style is directly related to both high fashion and mainstream trends, the popular press only infrequently features informative articles on punk's role in the fashion cycles. Fairly common press pieces include biographies of fashion designers associated with punk and subculture such as Vivienne Westwood or Anna Sui, or the occasional spotlight on a punk musical artist with crossover appeal into fashion influence. These discuss the relationship of that individual and his or her designs to punk, but often do not have much room for diving into the symbolism and lineage of their designs within broader social contexts. Westwood has received the most attention on this subject as an innovator of punk style, but profiles of her infrequently go into how punk style has morphed in numerous ways in subsequent years, and anyway her career has expanded in a multitude of directions.

Fig. 1.3   Red parachute top, Artificial Eye Kensington Market, a Seditionaries copy from approximately 1979 (copyright the Contemporary Wardrobe Collection, photograph Roger K. Burton).

In general, in fashion research, punk is often mentioned in passing as an influence, even though it is clearly relevant when studying an array of trends and visible in so many clothing styles that reinvent themselves cycle after cycle. Punk dress products are rarely analyzed even though they are regularly incorporated into many aspects of contemporary fashion and are also controversial for their possible disjuncture from their original intent. Fashion analysis needs to enhance its understanding of the punk styles often ingrained within fashion imagery as it is frequently used a tool, knowingly or not, to sell products and to revive designs through its movement around the always turning fashion cycle. The Metropolitan Museum of Art's 2013 *Punk* exhibition attempted to make this connection. Punk literature needs to address the importance of visuals, the material culture, and the embodiment that accompanies subcultural participation and often contributes to its empowerment. In fact, a third arena from which it is often excluded and needs further inclusion is social research, both academic and popular, as dress effects our lives in an infinite number of ways and yet is so often taken for granted. Dress is part of all we do, from identity formation and expression to design and innovation to finance and consumer behavior. Yet when studying social and individual behaviors, dress, in this case punk dress, is often overlooked.

The Literature: Fashion Needs to Get Attention in Punk Research

Upon completion of the research for this book, I evaluated why the study of punk style is often limited, and I found some distinct potential reasons. In the subculture's own memory of itself, and in documenters' efforts to catalog it, dress has been overshadowed for a few reasons. First, as with anything, when things are documented, certain biases rise to the top and are preserved for posterity. These representations are not always inaccurate, perhaps coming from a less-than-investigative journalist, or the scope may be incomplete, perhaps from a musician's memoir. Some writings attempt to understand or reflect on prevailing opinions within punk, or at least what are perceived as dominant concepts. They also are affected by strong outsider opinions about punk, such as those developed through media portrayals. Some representations of punk are unfortunately neglectful over aspects of the subculture that have proven through longevity and influence to be of valuable contribution to the maintenance of the lifestyle.

This seems curious, as punk started and continues to have a many-pronged critique of mainstream culture, and yet only its musical heritage has gotten sufficient page space, by the volumes. Some of the other prongs, including how one lives out daily life, have received analytical attention such as interiors, nutrition, business, and consumerism. Each of these components has garnered mass-market books and academic journal articles, yet surprisingly dress has not, even though many look to dress as a key instant signifier of punk. Some individuals who were present at the start of punk, such as Marco Pirroni, would argue the fashion of punk, at least in the United Kingdom, was a driving force behind its existence, and that music and even "community" were secondary concepts that evolved out of the visual form of expression (Interview with author, 2009).

Second, in historical and critical discussions of punk, fashion is thought of as a feminine art and punk is often thought of as a boys' club. This is a not uncommon belief of those within the scene and the analysts writing about it. The aggression of the music, the clothes, the art, and the anti-hegemonic attitudes is seen as tough and challenging, too much so for girls. Consequently, the hearty amount of literature dedicated to women's experiences in punk deal at least in part with their challenges regarding acceptance and extraordinary treatment (both good and bad). Punk culture is often perceived as a gathering of abnormal outsiders, yet norms do develop within the community. An example is that within these norms it is commonly unacceptable for a woman to embrace traditional notions of femininity and still be wholeheartedly punk.

Similar conclusions have been drawn regarding homosexuality in the punk scene and the challenged relationship of queer culture and punk culture with their parallels and contradictions. Hence, the brutish force perceived to drive punk's momentum is in opposition to fey perceptions of style, fashion, and interest in such. A thoughtful discussion of dress in some ways contradicts the inherently masculine slant of punk attitudes, history, and protocols. Thus it is possible that a rejection of fashion punk, meaning those who seem insincere as well as those who dress like they are trying too hard with the flamboyance of British punk-inspired style, may seem to be investing too much time in one's hair, styling, and makeup, which does not gel well with some facets of punk, particularly some of the more masculine and/or aggressive subgenres. While not necessarily openly or intentionally openly homophobic or misogynistic, punk's at times overt masculinity thematically is an awkward match with the iconic style's attention-grabbing look that indicates an obvious preference for self-attention to grooming and colorful appearances.

A third possible reason for the lack of discourse about punk dress is that for some, a punk is not supposed to be concerned with the thoughts and judgments of others—instead punk is often a critique of the viewer, a rejection of common fashion, or a form of antifashion. Therefore, common perceptions portray fashion as solely rooted in shallow acts of making a good impression. This perception, coupled with the blatant consumerism linked to notions of fashion or being fashionable seemingly contradicts many of punk's edicts. However, this perception of caring about fashion does not take into account analytical studies of "dress" separate from runway lines or mainstream trends. Nor does it take into account a wearer's empowerment in dress behaviors as a form of lifestyle choice and expression, in the manner of any other repetitive and important facet of life. This tactic of caring about dress evaluates the garment's form as well as its cultural significance and may be completely removed from popular perceptions of fashion leaning toward vanity or social compliance.

A final reason that emerged as to why punk style gets sparse critical attention is the notion of individuals versus groups. Since much of the collective memory formed regarding punk is coalesced around events, historians as well as scene insiders express varied opinions about whether punk was always considered a community, or whether individuals and small groups of friends are lumped together to create a larger subculture with ties that are actually thin. This confused take on punk as primarily a community is related to its conflicted relationship with fashion. While there are community events and a sense of shared community through common appreciation of art, music, and lifestyle choices as well as a shared history, individual experiences shape each participant. Hence, to study punk style is to study both the group take on things and the individual take on things, as punk is both a group and an individual lifestyle choice. This is not dissimilar to being religious, where overall doctrine and background functions parallel to personal experiences and a personal identity. The outcome is a unique spin on life, and in this case on style, specifically punk style.

Punk style is displayed not only within the context of the group environment, but frequently outside of it, in everyday life; challenging employers, family members, social constructs, and beauty standards. Thus the relevance of punk style permeates all aspects of its participants' lives, as well as others affected by it, and yet it is often not included in studies pertaining to these other aspects of life. While the exact clothes may change and be flexible because of differing demographics or contexts, there is often a commitment attached to punk dress through the permanence or semi-permanence of tattoos, hairstyles, piercings, and other lasting dress components including posture, bathing habits, and overall argot.

Punk is about style, and more so lifestyle, as much or more than about the sonic boom that is the music, even though the music and behaviors related to it get the bulk of attention in the literature. The fashion is personal and the body is a site of political and social commentary. The aesthetic choices of dress can scream as loud as any lead singer, in the form of bondage pants or blue hair, or whisper subtle secrets to a compatriot styled in a hidden piercing or an obscure band logo on a book bag. The fashion is often an entrée into expression of punk ideologies, and as punks age they may no longer as blatantly express that visually as they did in their youth, but often subtle cues stick with them for the long haul.

While the sentiment often incorporated into playing punk music is that anyone can do it, you still need the instruments (or these days at least computer software) and often others to share in the building of the experience through compatriots to play with and to. In fashion, however, anything you might wear can be reshaped through aesthetic choices, be it layers, or asymmetry, or ripping it up, or clashing your colors, and you can look punk. A goal is to be different from the norm and therefore confrontational to the viewer while proving thought provoking. Fashion is even more egalitarian as we all dress in some manner; even the naked have made dress behavior choices. It is individualistic, and allows virtually anyone to participate in the group behavior and also add his or her own interpretations and innovations. There are always more fans than there are members of the bands, and a community is made up of an array of participants shaping it in varied ways. It is valuable to document punk dress in an attempt to capture the robust and complete vision of the punk experience, as texts on other facets of punk lifestyles have attempted. This book strives to thoughtfully open these discussions.

Methodology for This Book

The foundation of this book is built on an array of research projects and methods. For the book specifically there was a great deal of content analysis and literature reviewed, and visits to personal and institutional punk-style costume collections in the United States and London, England. I also performed numerous formal and informal interviews and discussions, including with individuals who have actively participated in the punk subculture and about issues related to punk style ranging from mid-1970s London to the contemporary midwestern United States. The book also draws on primary and secondary studies I have worked on since 1996 on the subject of punk style, as well as on tertiary subjects such as other subcultures, designers, and trends. These have included literature reviews and historical analysis of urban street gangs, skinheads (neo-Nazi and nonracist), hair coloring and dye producers Tish and Snooky, black leather jackets, female music performers' appearances, the contemporary craft movement, black-colored apparel, and the style of seminal punk band the Ramones, among others.

In addition to those sources, a large portion of this book is drawn from my doctoral dissertation that asked: *"What are punk individuals' experiences concerning the apparel body construct for their workplace environments?"* This study is framed from the wearer's point of view to understand the individual's own concerns of his or her particular aesthetic process and the dress forms' relationship to varied identities within his or her overall self. The procedure to collect and analyze this data consisted of a series of steps. First, a pilot study focus group of five self-identified punks known to the researcher gathered to discuss the subject matter and my next steps were constructed based on those findings. Next, over 200 respondents answered a public open call and partook in a web-based survey to gather general information on the topic. This served as pre-identification to determine who would be good candidates for a long-form interview. The survey asked basic questions about punk and nonpunk (mostly workplace) experiences, dress behaviors, and demographics to gain insight on respondents' identity expression. Questions were conceived to learn more about the specific dress objects, body modifications, and behaviors the participant associates with punk and with nonpunk, especially in regard to jobs. Also included were questions aimed to gain information on how those dress choices are learned, performed, and creatively changed for punk and nonpunk environments. Once this data was reviewed a representative sample was selected for longer interviews.

The next step was to interview twenty individuals. The one-to-two-hour interviews were digitally audio taped and took place at coffeehouses and the interviewees' homes. The interview questions were similar to the survey in that they focused on background information on the interviewees' punk and nonpunk experiences, highlighting dress behaviors. The discussion topics covered the interviewees' punk dress history, work dress history, and the relationship between their punk and nonpunk dress. The in-depth interview format provided the opportunity to discuss interviewees' dress behaviors at length. Since participants were self-identified punks, they were each asked to clarify his or her definition of punk dress, what punk dress means, how he or she uses punk dress in relation to identity expression, and how punk dress relates to other aspects of his or her life. They also physically displayed and described some dress pieces and ensembles that represent their punk and nonpunk dress, and this portion of the discussion was captured through digital video.

The interviewees were aged twenty-six to forty-five and live in the areas of Chicago, Minneapolis-St. Paul, and metropolitan Detroit. All have been involved with punk since adolescence or early adulthood. Their personal punk styles ranged throughout the various subgenres of punk, including such visual signifiers as numerous tattoos and piercings, all-black attire, T-shirts with band logos paired with jeans, short-length skirts with thick-soled shoes, shaved heads, handmade or repurposed items, and chunky silver accessories including padlocks, pyramid-studded items, and bullets. Their professions range from business and law to education and the arts, among others, and their involvement in punk included playing in bands, writing zines/blogs, organizing punk events, and maintaining relationships with other members of the scene.

Through their responses it could be determined that they do feel dress is an expression of identity, although they do have mixed responses on how strongly. A greater number of interviewees use dress to express punk than use dress to express their nonpunk roles in life. However, the majority responded that they do try to look "appropriate" for contexts such as their workplace and that there are some punk garments they would and would not wear in nonpunk contexts.

In contrast with a great deal of previous literature on subcultural and/or punk style, this research focused on punks' own interpretation of themselves, rather than a third-party viewer's take on punk. There was the inclusion of many quotes to allow the respondents' voices to be heard, with limited interpretation on my part. I interpreted as much as possible from their point of view. This included not defining who can self-identify as punk, or what is punk dress, and letting them have long answers, only injecting my insider perspective when needed, and allowing the literature references to merge with emergent themes rather than force the data into the literature. The interpretation truly blossomed out of their responses.

Identity expression through dress is a form of complex storytelling. Observations of actual dress objects and witnessing the manner in which they are worn provided more thorough information than had I solely done an oral interview. This visual representation, in conjunction with their oral descriptions, facilitates a clearer grasp of how the individual perceives the object's design symbolism. This combination provides useful insight into punk style and creates an understanding into how singular garments might be used in differing applications and environments to signify varied ideas related to identity expression.

To differentiate between primary and secondary research, some references will be listed by first name and some by last name depending on the level of familiarity. To highlight the interviews with contemporary self-identified punks, as well as to provide some anonymity, their quotes will be referred to by first name. Excerpts from interviews I performed with topical experts, such as historians and punks from past eras, will also be referred to by the first name of the interviewee.[4] Literature citations and quotations pulled from other texts will be indicated by that author's full or last name.

After transcription the interviews were coded using the TAMS program.[5] This was done to decipher themes by repetition in the phrasing of respondents' answers to questions. In addition to this coding procedure to decipher important themes, interviews were reviewed case by case repeatedly to make sure no context or emphasis was lost in the coding process.

Fig. 1.4   Unisex black leather belt with metal pyramid studs (copyright Monica Sklar and Harlo Petoskey).

The software was a great organizational tool and highlighted themes I may not have identified if I was simply reading through and not trying to do the manual coding. Also, it is a method of forced objectivity to code everything rather than searching for themes that are potentially informed by any researcher bias I may have. Being a self-identified punk was helpful to understanding the language used, such as slang, the references made to bands, eras, and niche subject matter, and the potential implications of the findings, but it did not alter the data itself. Thus, whatever emerged as dominant themes from the data was not caused by my bias, and only helped by using it for clarity.

Upon completion of gathering and coding the interview materials, the audio and visual portions were compared with the literature review and my personal knowledge of punk to evaluate dress behaviors. Themes were determined based on repetition used in the responses by the interviewees, such as frequent use of the same words, phrases, and ideas. The various sources of material for this book were combined and compared to shape an analysis of punk style.

An Insider's Perspective

In the process of reviewing existing literature on punk style it became apparent that research from outsiders often struggled when it came to accuracy and getting deep inside the topic. Thus those projects feature points of view that come from the wearer and also the researcher in the analysis of the dress. Some would claim a researcher's mindset should not embody the scholarship, pointing toward objectivity as a key aspect of research. However, others would argue that a researcher's bias is always present in some manner and that acknowledging this bias in the research and writing process is a more truthful representation of how research develops (Finley 2003). Researcher bias is not necessarily a negative. Instead, if recognized it can serve as a further route to knowledge. With discussions of subcultural individuals and communities it is valuable that I have an "in" that an outside researcher may not. In the case of an insular group, some knowledge base regarding the content was optimal because often those within said communities will not share openly with an outsider and/or outsiders will not have a full understanding of what is being discussed.

I must be transparent about my own investment and experiences with punk culture as the researcher of this analysis, and accept how my biases affect this text. College rock and 1980s new wave were dominant forms of listening in my early teens, which would migrate into basement shows of punk and alternative bands. Sixties soul music, especially Motown and early girl groups, were always part of the mix as well (I grew up in metropolitan Detroit), and this interest (along with the new wave electronics) would transform itself into dance music with the corresponding raves and club nights. Both of these lines of interest were richly steeped in conscientious dress choices and corresponded with my passion for the do-it-yourself world of underground punk and later for tracing punk's history.

As I aged and dove deeper into contemporary punk, I focused primarily on the 1990s hardcore, straight edge, Riot Grrrl, and emo scenes (mostly out of the Midwest, East Coast, and southeastern United States), but also dabbled in an array of related subcultures. Detroit did have division of scenes, but also many overlapping communities and centralized hangout spots where individuals from goth, mod, rockabilly, hardcore punk, and garage rock[6] may all be bowling, drinking, admiring fine art, watching a fashion show, or rocking out to a favorite band together.

I went on to try my hand as a drummer and then a singer in a few short-lived and rarely publicly seen bands. My more active role was to co-organize large-scale events of punk bands and activities, as well as to be a frequent attendee at events. I always maintained enthusiasm for the aesthetic component, and did many jobs as a wardrobe stylist in the scene. Most punk bands do not use a stylist, but when some garage rock, ska, and more visually inclined groups began to gain wider audiences, my services were called upon to help perfect the look. I would later go on to manage and do public relations for bands and organize fashion shows, and through all of this became friends with individuals from around the country in all aspects of punk subculture; not just music kids, but political activists, event planners, fashionistas, artists, writers, and people who somehow incorporated punk into some aspect of their lifestyle. I immersed myself in the literature about the history of punk long before academia took its hold on me, and I could not get enough knowledge about the personalities, motivations, and social and artistic movements that fall under the umbrella of punk. The fun yet complex and confrontational components grabbed me

Fig. 1.5 Hooded sweatshirt, 1997. It was found left behind after a punk music festival co-organized by the author, and was already altered at the side seams by its previous owner to lay flat at the waistline. The author added "punk rock is not just for your boyfriend" on a handmade, silk-screened patch, which was purchased at a different punk women's festival and safety pinned on the lower back (copyright Monica Sklar and Harlo Petoskey).

and have never let go. And my own diversity of experience within subculture vastly influenced my positions and my forthcoming research path.

I believe my status as someone who self-identifies with the punk subculture affected how the interviewees for this research addressed me and it was reflected in my ability to comprehend their responses to my questions. I understood their casual language about subcultural brands, bands, and events, and I was able to include this knowledge in this book to provide clarity for the reader. Also, offhand comments such as "you know ..." meant interviewees were most likely comfortable to talk with me in a manner they may not have with an outsider. An outsider may have worked to get them to open up as readily and have had challenges analyzing the information. Furthermore, when I review research on this topic I have a sense of background and context to increase my understanding of the material.

Being an insider is not a perfect system, as there is vast room for individuality in dress and consequently my misinterpretation of meaning. The ability, however, to decipher some of the codes and design symbolism (Caplan 2005) is at least a worthwhile start of the discussion. I understand the specifics of the designs and can comprehend the vernacular slang and jargon that exist within a scene. In the writing of this book, I believe my background consequently affected the research in a positive way. I know, or know how to find out, what the one-inch button logo refers to, the history of the band silk screened on a patch, how much those boots cost, and where and when popularity rose for safety pins as jewelry or white headbands worn over short bleach blonde hair. There are greater social and aesthetic implications about those symbols beyond their direct ties to a few people's style choices or a band and its fans. Therefore, I have constructively utilized my biases to best understand this topic and made every effort not to make unfounded assumptions. I think I was able to use my biases to help and not hinder the research, and by revealing it early on both in this document and to the interviewees there are no hidden agendas or unrealistic expectations of objectivity. But the literature research, especially the TAMS coding, did balance any preconceived notions I may have had or personal influences that could have colored my analysis. Researcher reflection is useful to combine related ideas under umbrella concepts that may have seemed disparate to someone unaware of punk or dress concepts. The balance is in blending this punk attitude with ideas from an academic viewpoint. I am also able to step back and holistically unite ideas to answer the research questions as a scholar of dress, design, and social theory.

Conclusions

The popular press often creates a punk caricature reducing dress to a costume rather than a significant part of a lifestyle filled with humor, anger, art, and practical functionality. Punk style encompasses a broad range of ideas. This book explores these through a comprehensive method that includes a historical overview; a discussion of influences, motivations, and societal impact; a review of merchandising and fashion cycles; and a look to potential future directions of punk style. As punk continues to grow and remain a strong subculture through Internet use, buying power, and designers and others appropriating its styles, it is important to document and better understand the group itself.

Punk Style Past and Present

Quite a few summers ago I went on a vacation that included a tour of Amish country in the eastern United States. I paid to take the tour and glimpse what Amish life was all about. Something grabbed me about a group of content outsiders who cling to their ideals, yet they, or perhaps just those who observe them, wrestle with how they fit into the broader contemporary society.

On this sunny day, the tour was packed and I rode up front in the horse-drawn buggy, sitting with the Amish man who served as our guide. I was probably dressed in my typical casual fashion for these summer vacations—a mix of capri pants with a T-shirt or tank top that represents a retro style or often a band. My dark, curly hair and straight bangs were often dyed with vibrantly contrasting Crayola-colored highlights, and my accessories were frequently plentiful, including an eyebrow piercing.

The carriage took us around the property, and after completing the rounds, the guide answered the questions of those of us on the tour about Amish life and heritage. He turned to me and said he had *his own* cultural question. He explained he often went into the heavily populated nearby town and saw people dressed "like me" and that he did not understand it. What is that all about? I chuckled, saying I felt the same way about the Amish, which is why I paid to go on the tour. After our Hallmark-esque moment of cultural common ground, I attempted to give him his own snapshot audio tour through punk style history and motivations.

This encounter resonated with me long after that fleeting afternoon. I thought about why some cultures become tourist attractions and hold such fascination for outsiders, while others, like punk culture, are almost chastised for maintaining a specific aesthetic, and historical institutions such as museums are shunned for acknowledging the place of popular culture, counterculture, and avant-garde design within Western heritage.[1] Additionally, I have considered concepts including why some groups remain traditional while others are constantly progressive, how the design symbols of something seemingly mundane (such as the shape of a man's facial hair) are powerfully meaningful, and why some societies and contexts prioritize aesthetic individuality while others promote conformity. It is these types of questions that drive a study of punk style.

What Is Punk Style?

What is punk dress and how did it get that way? For some punk style is an obvious reference to green mohawk hair, a leather jacket, plaid pants, and combat boots. For others it is an oversized hooded sweatshirt and jeans, clean white shoes, and a wallet chain. Some say it is a current caricature of a dead movement while others say it is an ever evolving shape shifter.

Punk style in fact can be all of those things and everything in between. It has signature characteristics and flexibility in how its voice is articulated visually. Although it is different to varied eyes, it is possible to deconstruct the many components of punk style and to trace some of the history of those design choices to provide a lineage for what came to be known as punk style by combining material from a host of literature sources, as well as collection visits, and, most important, interviews with self-identified punks past and present.

Today, punk style has a forty-year history, with a host of influences and a myriad of characteristic pieces that make up the look, as well as flexibility to include new components. Origins of the key aspects of punk style—which include the color black; heavy accessories; boots; clothing that is tattered and manipulated; piercings; tattoos; unnatural hair colors; facial hair; band logos; and jeans, T-shirts, and hooded sweatshirts—have become fragmented and fractured through various subgenres under the punk umbrella.

This form of dress was not created in a vacuum. A merger of bricolage, appropriation, creativity, innovation, and circumstance birthed punk style and continues to reinvent it. Using existing objects in new ways is a core idea of punk. This is done whether the fresh approach is to reshape the design to suit one's own need, or to subvert its original meaning through changing the context or political spirit of the object (Leblanc 1999). It has always reflected on the context around it to innovate new styles and reconfigure existing ideas. Punk style developed differently than the tangible manifestation of other subcultures in its use of an almost haphazard manner of taking in anything suitable for that momentary burst of creativity, expression, or performance on and off stage. Typically subcultures exhibit caution in their selection of dress items, and dress behaviors were guided by finite rules of what could be included (Polhemus 1994). This is not to say the appropriation punks employed lacked thoughtfulness in use of the source material, as there was often critique rooted within the choices, but the pantheon of choices to draw from was not limited. Eventually, punk style would be complicated as this technique of using whatever was around that was pleasing merged with new generations of punks paying respect to the first generation, who in part were thoughtful about their choices and were simply experimenting.

As punk style started in the 1970s, it was a reaction to the society around it, an artistic movement of the people within it, and it heavily reflected the subcultures predating and surrounding it. Punk style drew from many sources pulled together to represent cohesion of similar ideas, even if they did not outwardly look the same because of individual stylistic interpretations. Homage is a significant aspect of punk and a part of why there are so many different looks in punk today. This admiration can be for a subculture or movement of the past, or it can be for a contemporary lifestyle one wishes to associate with. Punks align themselves with varied aspects of punk's past, not just the iconic parts. Within punk, maintaining knowledge of a garment's past is often a challenge, and the homage is sometimes a stylistic nod without historical context. Other times it is less a reference to the exact nature of the original item in use than it is a similar attitude or necessity, such as budget or functionality. A dirty appearance and steel-toed Dr. Martens boots are examples.

Punk by Wearer Definition

The moniker *punk* is most accurate when self-identified because of the infinite variation in how it is expressed. There is community, and thus there are common looks, but punk is also fundamentally implanted within a wearer's definition of its existence. Much of what composes punk style is in the wearer's juxtaposition of garments and accessories put together for aesthetic preferences and sociocultural cues. How an ensemble is put together and how each piece is worn is all-important in composing a punk style. Chrissy describes her opinion on this: "I think the way that you put things together and sometimes unconventionally … or maybe accessorizing them maybe changes the way they're interpreted. And maybe that's more of my style now by taking those things and making them what I want them to be." In a sense, punk style is mostly designated by wearer definition. However, there are basic aesthetic components that tend to make up the foundation of punk style.

A punk style is composed in multiple ways. To accomplish this one can create clothing from scratch, make adaptations to existing attire, or simply take ready-to-wear and position the items together to develop the punk style. Denise discussed how her punk style is a self-creation from mainstream sources:

> I'm not shopping at anyplace special. I'm shopping at Kohl's, at Target, at Marshall's, at TJ Maxx. Wherever. I'm not going to any particular place that specializes, like Hot Topic or whatever … not going anyplace specifically. So I find something that appeals to me because of the different kind of shape it has or some sort of, the design of it itself. And then it is usually with the other accessories that makes it, that gives it a little extra flair.

Sometimes just the way items that would typically be considered nonpunk are positioned together in ensembles makes the entire look appear punk by relating the parts to the whole (DeLong 1998). An innocuous example would be dark colors and a slim-fitting T-shirt with jeans and revealed sleeve tattoos. While the items are conventional or even mundane, when placed together and revealing body modifications they take on a punk appearance. Punk interviewee Brian elaborates with a personal example: "I guess when you put it all together with the baseball cap and the jeans and the shoes, I have a plain plaid shirt that could be considered punk now. You roll up the sleeves so some of your tattoos show. It's a plain plaid shirt so I wouldn't say it's a punk shirt, but I guess it becomes that way when you put it all together." Similarly, choice of specific brands such as mod-punk favorite Fred Perry can take conventional items like a three-button collared shirt and tweak them to make them recognizable to insiders as cues to subcultural involvement.

Sometimes the connection of context and the details of the outfit can make all the difference in whether something comes across as punk. Mainstream items worn in punk contexts or by someone who identifies as punk can change the symbolism of an item. Ben commented:

> One could wear an ironic T-shirt, like an old church picnic T-shirt that somebody got at a thrift store ... Now on a punk person in a completely different setting, it becomes a punk rock T-shirt. Just by the context in which they're wearing it.

Additionally, context can change the purpose of items, and they can be reassigned as appropriate in different environments based on how they are accessorized and how much the outfit focuses on the item. Rachel described the transformation between her appearance for work and nonwork situations:

> I think sometimes it [punk] is more the way you combine things. Like a particular shirt, if I wore it to work, I'd pull it up on my shoulders ... But if I weren't wearing it to work, I'd have a tank top underneath it with red straps and it would be down on my shoulders and I'd have huge earrings. So it is the combination, it is the whole look. I might use more product in my hair and make it more messy. Things like that, that to me would push me into, make it a little edgier ... I could wear more eyeliner. Add just a little bit of this and that and it ends up looking very, very different.

Aesthetic Components of Punk Style

Certain aesthetic components are frequently utilized even within the individual interpretations constructing a punk look. Through the manipulation of these aesthetics, such as color choices or proportion of the garments on the body, an individual can turn disparate items into a punk appearance and align with specific aspects of punk culture, its long history, and its contemporary array of subgenres. The following are some of the most common aesthetic components.

Fig. 2.1 Woman wearing a composite of multiple punk aesthetic components (copyright Getty, photographer Ryan McVay, collection Stockbyte).

Oppositional Shapes

Punk shapes often tend to be in opposition to one another. The look may have hard edges, defined lines through the cut of the silhouette and the trim such as zippers, and chunky, oversized pieces mixed with undersized tight garments. Mainstream shapes, with the lines and drape that compose them, may include softer edges such as twin sets for women, smaller features such as delicate jewelry and shoes, and equal proportions such as neat suits rather than strong distinctions of large and small. Punk does include some rounded edges and flowing shapes, such as loose T-shirts and baggy denim pants, but also lots of harsh, sharp lines of stripes and leathers and denser fabrics that appear too heavy to be fluid, even when the actual edge of the garment is rounded.

The acceptable proportions for punk attire as compared to nonpunk attire differ, and the punks expressed discomfort when wearing conventionally mainstream proportions. Punks want things that fit properly within the parameters of an accepted punk aesthetic, and are less concerned about the fit of their clothing in nonpunk contexts.

Garments for nonpunk contexts may appear dowdy or ill fitting in punk, even if to the mainstream eye there are no fit issues, and from that point of view the proportions of punk style are off. Trends in punk such as ultra-skinny jeans, very baggy jeans, tight baby doll T-shirts, and layered and asymmetrical clothes may not appear to have proportions and fit thoughtfully attended to, however it is precisely the opposite. Some punks express that it is burdensome to wear conventional Western proportions, as they find joy in the differentiation that comes with an unconventional appearance.

Katie adds that how she mixes items together changes the meaning of each item when they are part of an entire look:

> I think maybe just with you know how you do your hair, or sometimes when my tattoo shows that maybe makes it look a little more [punk]. So I try to take something that could maybe be pretty but then make it look like rougher, a little bit. And I use it to maybe downplay the prettiness of it in a sense; I kind of like to take something nice and then take something the opposite and add them together.

Patterns and Iconography

Distinct patterns and iconography have become ingrained in punk style. Patterns can pay tribute to broadly influential time periods of the past. Examples such as hound's-tooth, check, and stripes are frequently seen in punk attire. There is some overlap in pattern usage between punk and nonpunk contexts. Many patterns are greatly linked to proportion and context, while some colors are virtually off limits in punk. Some patterns, such as florals, are seen with limited frequency. Furthermore, multiple patterns worn together can compose a punk style because the chaos and confusion is harsh on the eye.

Iconography is another form of punk style when it is found in band logos or subversive images such as a skull and crossbones. In a nonpunk context one can use many of the same patterns, but in more subtle ways and rarely with the goal of being hard on the eye through contrasting patterns or bright colors in the patterns. Patterns geared more to the mainstream and not toward punk use florals and pinstripes, for example, for cues that read as feminine, nonconfrontational, or conservative.

One of the most well-known examples of an iconic pattern in punk is the use of plaid or tartan. The color palate and pattern of tartan was a symbol of clans and community as well as rebelliousness. In the years after its inception it became familiar in British culture. After clothing lines inspired by Teddy Boys and Fetish wear, Vivienne Westwood and Malcolm McLaren wanted to lean toward high fashion and create looks that were a thorough package of design and discontent, which is where tartan came in. Jonathan Faiers explained:

> The history of tartan as a fabric expressive of revolt and opposition, its remarkable status as a cloth outlawed by the English and its association with royalty made it the perfect

textile for a range of clothing that aimed to make anarchy, alienation, and indeed sedition wearable, and for dressing the voice of this challenging position: The Sex Pistols. (2008: 98)

When they began their Seditionaries clothing line in 1976, Westwood and McLaren's use of tartan brought back to the forefront the idea of tartan as a distinguishing and unifying symbol of a particular group of people (in this case punks), as well as its association as a cloth of those fighting a battle. These ideas solidified the use of plaid as a symbol of punk.

Westwood's employment of tartan was avant-garde at its finest, and the garments were unwearable for most, although punks enjoyed the styling of the bondage pants and complicated tops. However, this renewed interest in tartan as an expression of dissent would become indelible, and it was easily repackaged in more accessible forms by retailers and designers, as well as by punk wearers through pillaging secondhand shops and their own family wardrobes. Tartan would become a punk staple seen in miniskirts, bum flaps, and patches with silk-screened band logos atop. This new use of plaid in punk became its own form of clan representation (Faiers 2008). It was linked not only to Westwood's shop and the bands and community she aligned with, but also the spirit of rebellion she was appropriating.

This "marketing of England's history of colonial atrocities" (Faiers 2008: 98) would be thinned through the years as tartan became so commonplace it lost some of its rebellious appeal, becoming primarily recognized as the conservative staple it simultaneously was. As is true of most things subcultural, especially those brought to the surface through a designer, tartan found its way into the mainstream consciousness, and the original intent of the innovator was watered down over time, thus repositioning tartan as a go-with-everything style that lacks some of its initial verve. This is not the only item from punk style with multiple layers of inspiration built in, but as they grow and change they maintain that for some and lose it for others, especially when the items are widely available or reappropriated to begin with. That said, in some contexts, it is still brash to be seen in a bold plaid pattern, especially in volume such as in pants. Whether it is the symbolism behind the pattern, or the aesthetics of its colorful palette, tartan is an example of how a pattern or iconography can have a strong significant in punk style.

Color

Color is another important concept in punk aesthetics and has tighter parameters of what is acceptable to punks than patterns. Color is an effective tool to communicate mood, identity, and alignment with ideas and other people, and is a source of creative expression. Punk colors tended to be darker shades, especially black, with deep shades of navy, green, and gray. Brights are incorporated when the color is so neon it can be deemed almost obnoxious. Red is another useful accent color that is commonly seen. Punks use their dark and contrasting palette to express a place in the world and an ideology through aesthetics. Dark attire is aggressive, mysterious, shadowy, and artistically sophisticated, and the negative and powerful associations with the color black, with all its absorption qualities, give off the desired effect. This is compared to the bright clean appearance of white with its pure and innocent connotations and pastels and their soothing agreeability, even passivity. However some punks, such as those who follow the straight edge lifestyle,[2] would use white symbolically to represent purity, whether they knew they were doing it or not (Sklar and Michel 2012).

There are also functional characteristics to dressing dark in a culture where some of its members eschew washing as lifestyle, and items that are well worn can be revered for their commitment. Dark colors handle this kind of wear and tear better than light shades. Earthy tones do not suit a punk mentality as successfully, as thematically punk is a culture of the people and the street, not the trees and land. Black and metallics reflect urban architecture, the facets of machinery and buildings and the system that chains one down, but also tools with which one can build and repair (Sklar and Michel 2012).

Texture

Whether a garment is perceived as punk is also related to the way objects feel to the touch and the way they appear that they may feel. Some textures, including tweed and corduroy, cross over between punk and nonpunk contexts. Others, however, remain strictly geared toward only one world or the other. Examples include leather being relegated to punk, whereas woven synthetics, especially for pants, were acceptable only in a nonpunk context such as a business office.

The aesthetic elements of certain punk styles are still worn, and mostly retain their original design symbolism, while other aesthetic elements of punk expression are flexible, adjusting to suit the era or the individual. Skateboarders and anarchist punks may share metal-studded belts, dyed hair, and antiauthoritarian slogans on T-shirts, but otherwise their wardrobes have developed in divergent ways in everything from the color palette to the textures to the line and proportion of the garments. If each subgenre of punk has created a style that best represents its lifestyle, what about the original belt with its leather and metal attachments and the vibrant and unnatural hair color represents core punk values both groups share?

Thematic Components of Punk Style

With the aesthetics established, the themes that drive the look can be explored. Punk style is composed of thematic choices that are physical and cultural. These themes then take on visual and material manifestations. Some examples are as follows:

One of a Kind/DIY/Vintage

The idea of being unique resonates through many punk dress choices, differentiating from the mainstream and from each other. Punks want to be either socially accepted for their difference—the desire, in fact, which often initially led them to punk ideas and the punk community. Thus do-it-yourself, often referred to as "DIY," is vastly popular as a way to create unique appearances. This can be styling things in a way that one developed on his or her own, or creating items from scratch, or redoing items through embellishments and repurposing. Deconstructing denim jackets and then adding on patches of band logos, leopard trim, and/or metal studs is an example seen across the globe in punk style.

DIY is a strong tenet of punk that indicates freedom of thought, particularly regarding identity expression. This is not unique to punk, as crafting has had resurgence in recent years. The craft movement is aligned with punk in spirit but does not consist solely of those who would identify as punk. Furthermore, not all punks utilize

Fig. 2.2 Garage work jacket personalized with patches, pins, and sewn-on leopard collar (copyright Monica Sklar and Harlo Petoskey).

DIY methods to construct their apparel, as there are plenty of ready-made jeans and T-shirts worn. However even those premade garments can be a form of DIY because they will frequently be manually silk screened to have the logo of an independent band, or the image was designed by an individual rather than a corporation, or the image/text is antiauthoritarian.

Parallel to the concept of DIY in punk style is the active use and careful selection of vintage and used clothing. Dresses from the 1950s and 1960s, and 1970s and 1980s-style T-shirts, cardigans, and sweater vests may be repurposed by punks. Chrissy provided personal examples: "Repurposing a lot of things … wearing a lot of clothes that had been my mother's or my aunt's and when those didn't fit or weren't going to be turning them into something else … mixing 1950s and 1960s style and maybe even getting nerdier than most people would."

Zhac continued to share from her experiences:

> In the '80s it was much more about recycled clothing. And you could find a lot more cool stuff … I wore tights and skirts and whatever strange cool weird shirts I could find. I didn't really have a lot of money so a lot of it was from free boxes. I wore a lot of lingerie as outer clothing.

Recycling clothing in punk has multiple motivations including budget needs, expressing individuality through the rare finds at resale shops, the ease with which an older garment can be repurposed, and the quick route to expressing homage to previous styles and genres.

Distressed Apparel

For many punks distressed appearances are the norm. Punk clothing is often not pristine, with an allowance for rips, stains, and holes. Sometimes this comes out of lifestyle and budget necessity, and sometimes out of aesthetic choice, and frequently the initial motivation and the lingering aesthetic are cyclical and overlap in influence.

Jonathan explained:

> I wear a lot of torn-up shorts. You know I buy a pair of shorts or I'll buy a pair of pants and I'll just cut the bottom legs off … And I kind of just wear them over and over again. They all have holes on them … just everything's kind of more as I wear it, it's more ratty for a better term … Or tattered is a better word.

Dirty and worn-in clothes are acceptable within punk more so than mainstream fashion. This is often about functionality and budget, as well as a reaction to social mores. Some elements within punk, however, are quite polished, particularly those references to subcultures with a penchant for dressing up such as mod. However, dress up within punk walks a fine line between swagger, aspiration, and irony. Social concepts about dirt and moral worth pervade the use of a distressed appearance in punk style. The definition of dirt itself is up for debate with matter from the ground, the air, and the body all viewed in varying ways. Frequently, middle-class participants in subcultures present an unkempt appearance as an outward sign of their political, environmental, and social ideals that may blatantly differ from their upbringing, adding to the emphasis. There are many examples in society where the washed might judge the unwashed as lazy, immoral, or low class, but it is a true two-way equation because the unwashed can also have specific motivations that are potentially misunderstood. Masquelier (2005) argued that perhaps the idea of dirt as negative comes from basic social control issues. People want to be in control of themselves, and often others, and feel a sense of accomplishment and even superiority when there is a great deal of control. The downtrodden that lack facilities for washing, differing hygiene expectations, infants, the elderly, the infirm, and the mentally unstable that possibly cannot attend to or need assistance with bodily matters, all make another person feel in control. Sean explored the value of soiled clothes:

> A little bit more worn-in clothes. Always have holes in the jeans … in the wintertime, long underwear underneath the T-shirts. And in general, you can wear your punk clothes when you're not around a punk environment to get them to the certain spot. You know, wash your whites with your blacks to make sure that they're not too white. Especially your long underwear. You know you almost got to get them brown before you can put them on.

Some punks embrace tattered clothing and/or soiled hair and bodies in a one-two punch of not accepting the mainstream's standards of beauty and social status, and having so much control over oneself they can contentiously buck those notions without a loss of personal power because of their self-awareness and position of choice for this frame of dressing.

Body Modification

There are many forms of body modification, and truly all dress can fall within this category.[3] Using the phrase as it is commonly applied in subcultural terms, it refers mostly to marking the body through writing on it, tattoos, and piercing, including the stretching of ears and piercing a variety of places throughout the body (Featherstone 1999). Body modification extends to other forms such as branding, scarification, and implants that can be seen in punk but are less common in other styles. These modifications may serve as punk cues for identity and artistic expression, as well as to acknowledge and embrace social difference and to demonstrate scene involvement (Sweetman 1999).

Permanent and abundant body modification was not commonplace in the early years of punk. Temporary or minimal modifications such as a small number of tattoos and piercing in unusual places such as the nose or cheek with a crude implement like a safety pin were seen. Piercing beyond the Western traditional female lower earlobe started to become commonplace in the late 1980s and early 1990s, becoming very popular in the mid-1990s, and was often metal and in places like eyebrows, septum, and the tragus (inner ear cartilage). This modern trend of the counterculture adopting piercing as a signifier can be traced back to its use in gay culture after World War II, through the body expressions of Fakir Musafar, who popularized the notion of modern primitivism, and then to the opening of the first piercing studio, Gauntlet, in 1978. Visually referencing non-Western influences grew in acknowledgment, and decorative jewelry made from wood and stone were new accessories.

In Western culture, tattoos have always been aligned with counterculture when not linked to the military, and while they were present on the occasional punker who chose to get a little ink, it really took hold in punk in the 1990s, particularly in the skatepunk and hardcore realms of punk subgenres. Musician Henry Rollins of the

Fig. 2.3 Body modifications including tattoos and stretched earlobe piercings, London, 2012 (copyright PYMCA, photographer Marc Vallée).

band Black Flag (now a solo performer) and members of the New York band the Cro-mags are credited with helping to popularize "ink" in the punk subculture (Blush 2001). Temporary modifications can make a strong impression as well. The straight edge and Riot Grrrl movements have utilized writing on the body to signify personal control and communicate a message.

There is debate as to how edgy body modifications continue to be as they increase in mainstream popularity, but many punks still are adorned with them and feel they do represent punk ideas. The specific image of the tattoo, its placement on the body, and the context in which it was performed inform its perception as punk by wearers and viewers.

Radical Hair

Dramatically changing one's hair away from societal norms is one of the most common and accessible forms of body modification, yet also highly visually stimu-lating. A man using obvious dyes or a woman shaving her head bald are seen as transgressive. A variety of hairstyles that fall within punk style employ products including glue, egg whites, vegetable dyes, and lots of hairspray. All must withstand the rigors of a punk hairstyle's height, volume, and need to last through a sweaty, highly physical music show. A pompadour or beehive can allude to edgy youth of another era, evoking their coolness and transplanting it onto oneself.

Foremost in punk is the use of unnatural colors including blue, green, pink, and vibrant reds. The use of unnatural hair color as a pertinent part of punk dress indi-cates the embrace of a subversive differentiation from the norm, as well as a nod to the subculture's past. Hair color is also a route to be individually innovative with one's look in a temporary manner, promoting constant change, fun, and provocative flouting of convention. The hair dye and cosmetics brand Manic Panic was started in the 1970s by New York City sisters Tish and Snooky Bellomo. They understood the importance of hair, specifically hair color. With their creation of their seminal brand (they also had a boutique featuring punk fashions which was rare at the time), they revolutionized what colors were used in Western culture and brought business sense to the punk aesthetic, while adding fun, ease, and accessibility to the development of a rock look. Hair dying can be traced to ancient times, as well as throughout global cultures, and through the development of a late-twentieth-century brand aimed at punks they contributed to the Western acknowledgment of unusual hair color and broader beauty standards through the wide marketing and availability of their hair color and cosmetic products.

Caucasians donning dreadlocks, sometimes in a rainbow of colors, also can fall under punk style. This style was functional for the "crusty" punk set as washing and a presentation of disdain for conventional Western beauty and time spent on adorn-ment went along with that philosophy. Slinkard (2006) explained that, beginning in the 1950s, English ghettos were populated by immigrant Jamaicans "living in close proximity to lower class Britons—it is during this period and in these neighborhoods that youth from varying cultural backgrounds began to trade cultural ideals and aesthetics. The resulting mixtures were then re-appropriated by the developing punk subculture ... Overall, spirituality, rebellion, differentiation, as well as assimilation seem to be most prevalent means for adopting and wearing dreadlocks." By the 1980s, some salons—such as Hair Police in Minneapolis, a salon that innovated methods to dread and color Caucasian hair—were specifically catering to countercultures. With the Twin Cities a hotbed for internationally known punk music and activities, visibility of these styles spread.

Specific Accessories

Body modifications such as band tattoos and pink hair make a strong statement with their commitment to be seen in every context. Accessories can be the opposite, as they have flexibility in their use and can promote an ensemble to punk status loudly or quietly and their removal can strip that identity away visually. The use of accessories is a simple and often inexpensive way to express punk identity, and to have one's garments not be relegated to only certain contexts. Thus if punks wear classic basics, they can switch up accessories to transform their appearance, making their wardrobe go further. They can change up shoes and jewelry and switch from a workplace to a music show quickly. There is also a subtlety to accessories, more so than in whole styles that are ironically punk. Examples include neon or ripped fishnet tights, wallet chains, backpacks, piercing jewelry, and one-inch pins with logos and symbols. These little details can act as codes to be read by another punk as a sign of kinship. Katie described her choices in accessories: "I guess I would say that [punk] mainly it exists within my accessories. Because I think a lot of the stuff I have is pretty basic, like I'll have a black dress or just have like jeans and something. But I'll have really like heavy bags and boots and like jewelry." There are also cycles, the development of subgenres, and trends in punk, which can be expressed in terms of accessories incorporated over simple or classic styles; examples include Hare Krishna wooden beaded choker necklaces and 1950s-style eyeglasses.

For men, it can be the way facial hair is groomed. Excess hair can be seen as containing dirt because of its lack of trimness, or as a mask hiding one's expressions, or as aggressively masculine in its show of hair growth; therefore a man's facial hair has the potential to be seen as outside of the norm in an environment where clean shaven is preferred by viewers. Sean explained: "From a facial hair perspective ... Way back, it used to be goatees and those got too commonplace. Now it's really funny, it's like beards. [I'm] kind of unfortunately fitting the mold. I've got to have a beard, because that says you're a punk rocker. Which is very bizarre."

Another accessory common in punk style is small, metal studs in a pyramid shape affixed to belts, bracelets, collars of jackets—really anywhere. They have long been associated with rock and roll, and have been used in all sorts of countercultures. Their popularity within punk began when McLaren was interested in the fetishistic themes behind the heavy metal studs he discovered at a leather store catering to bikers. They lacked the delicate and fanciful fashion appeal of the day, and had an appealing rough presentation (Gorman 2010). This look would grow to include similar items such as spikes, bullets, and other metal embellishments.

Accessorizing can also highlight certain iconography of a band, an event, a political idea, or an organization, which then aligns the wearer to the ideas embedded within the logo. This is similar to the aesthetic concept of certain patterns and icons appearing punk. The placement of a selected image can quickly communicate a punk representation. An "X," presented generally in a thick black font, was used on clothing and in tattoos and written in Sharpie on the hands by those within the straight edge movement to clearly signify their commitment to the cause. This X represented those abstaining from intoxicants and sometimes even sex, having started as a sign that one was under eighteen at clubs, with the mantra popularized by those who felt kinship to the 1980s hardcore band Minor Threat's song entitled "Straight Edge." Harkening back to the X on the hands of those who were underage at a social venue and were marked unable to partake by bouncers, the self-written X signified a choice of abstinence and saying no by crossing something out. The 1987 Swatch brand watch with a

Fig. 2.4　Men's and women's punk-style bracelets (copyright Monica Sklar and Harlo Petoskey).

simple black X became quite collectable and desirable within that scene. Accessories can be a way for aging punks, who do not want to be so visually extreme anymore and want smaller references to punk, to express themselves. They want to expend less effort and money and thus the cues are inserted into otherwise conventional clothing.

Athletic Casual

Many contemporary punks utilize casual, toned-down apparel in their everyday appearance, reflecting a strategy of subtlety. Subgenres such as hardcore utilize this look with basketball jerseys with oversized jeans and white athletic shoes, and skatepunks (i.e., skateboarders) wear the logos of obscure bands on T-shirts with Dickies work pants and Converse shoes. Hooded sweatshirts, both pullover and zip up, are universally a part of this style and worn by men and women. This look is about comfort and utilitarianism, not about avant-garde experimentation or shocking confrontation. It is frequently a fairly clean, washed appearance, however some more worn-in versions still fall under this header. The proportions in the fit and silhouette range from extremely narrow to exaggeratedly baggy, and these aesthetic elements reflect different trends that are regional, time-period oriented, and represent small subgenres.

It also presents an image of effortless cool with less time spent on the highly exaggerated presentation of other punk styles, although in contrast there is great pride in the in-the-know details of what a logo may represent. This styling is built on accessibility, with a stereotypically masculine bent, whether it is a DIY T-shirt screening of band names or the ability to buy pieces at the local mall and position them together into a punk appearance. Form-fitting T-shirts evolved later to feminize the style.

Audra commented on her frequent use of T-shirts as a sign of being punk: "I would say I fall primarily into the hardcore punk category … I just have kind of the casual type of feminine pants that aren't super tight. And a whole lot of T-shirts with bands on them. Whether they're girlie tees or guy tees." T-shirts have a universal appeal because they are affordable, durable, and worn by all facets of society (Duffty and Gorman 2009). British label Wonder Workshop (wonderworkshop.co.uk) solidified the art of silk screening images onto jersey fabric in 1970, and its leopard-emblazoned and bejeweled Jimi Hendrix T-shirt became a favorite of glam rockers and helped usher in the T-shirt as a fashionable statement piece (Duffty and Gorman 2009). Wearing a T-shirt as a punk is not always about fashion creativity or standing out, but can be motivated by function in the T-shirt's ease and familiarity. Nate explained:

> I do it more casually now, so it's not as obvious. But I would say it's more in the band T-shirts I guess that I wear … I think I always look punk to somebody else who's into the music. They look at me and say OK, this person's one of us.

Nate expresses his interest and identity through the band names on his T-shirts, and Audra's feminine T-shirts can indicate punk to a knowing viewer. These T-shirts can even tip people off to whether someone is a poser depending on how popular the band is, how easy it is to obtain the garment, and what condition the shirt is in. Often the lesser known or shorter lived the band is or the more worn in the shirt the better. This display indicates deep knowledge of something insular, or that the garment is old or has been well worn, both of which signify high levels of commitment.

Shoes and Boots

Many types of shoes have a place in punk history. For the dressing-up versions of punk style, retro-style boots and shoes are often the choice. Pointy Winklepickers and sleek Beatle boots have a stylish air and Brothel creepers with their abundant soles stand tall with distinguished pride (Duffty and Gorman 2009); they are still made the way they have been since 1949 to the same lasts, chunky sole, pointed toe, and weave across the top. Sneakers are very popular in the dressing-down set, for the comfort, casual style, color choices, and timeless appearance that links them to generations of youth culture. Converse, often referred to by their style names of Chucks and All Stars, were the tennis shoe of youth throughout the twentieth century, and the Ramones were constantly seen in theirs, forever linking them to punk. Vans took their place in the lineage as skateboarding moved from mainstream in the 1970s to aggressive punk attitudes in the 1980s and beyond.

Chunky, oversized boots have universal appeal because in addition to comfort, they give an air of intimidation, symbolically solidifying their footing in this world as valid, not treading lightly but making a real stand that they cannot be messed with. Engineering boots are popular, and reflect power and industry, as does the free-wheeling nature of motorcycle boots (Duffty and Gorman 2009). The frequently black, dark, or metallic colors, the metal accessories like chains and buckles, rubber soles, and leather that compose the tough exteriors reflect an ability to withstand challenges. For women, this is in part relevant in contrast to the dainty and vulnerable high heels and similar styles that can indicate complying with societal limitations on gender presentations.

The brand of footwear most associated with punk is Dr. Martens. There is historic precedence with the often steel-toed Dr. Martens boots, and this theme has been carried through with various other styles including motorcycle boots and multi-buckled goth-inspired styles. The brand started in the 1940s as a comfortable yet functional option for military and work use. In 1960, the "1460" model went into production and became a staple of punk fashion. British skinheads of the 1960s played a large part in popularizing them among youth and subcultures as they frequently wore the boots that were "wrenched unwittingly from the workplace" (AirWair Limited 1999: 12).

Fig. 2.5   Dr. Martens 1460 boot (copyright Dr. Martens).

By the early 1970s, the subcultural associations were starting to solidify as Dr. Martens were known for "working class roots, its durability and apparent flexibility to change" (AirWair Limited 1999: 12) as they incorporated stylistic markers relevant to timely tastes and expanded functions. By the mid-1970s, the burgeoning punk scene was focused on individuality and flourished with the styles of Westwood and McLaren, as well as other punk designers who were highly limited because of availability and geography, with only a few shops catering to this new band of outsiders. Those unable to shop those routes would embrace the DIY option of resale shops and piecing together punk looks out of one's own closet. Uniformly appealing, though, were Dr. Martens, which were affordable, long lasting, and, most important, widely available and thus suited the needs of punks aesthetically, financially, and functionally (AirWair Limited 1999).

"In many senses the Dr. Martens 1460 was the anathema to much of what punk fashion stood for—many punks were unique, non-uniform, and so the 1460 [boot] was arguably the only item of punk gear that was of a standard design" (AirWair Limited 1999: 33). They looked great with drainpipe pants and vintage dresses and could withstand years of use and aggressive dancing, making them a budget win adored by men and women alike. They would fade from popularity for a while, but in the 1980s they would be revived by the California punk and hardcore scenes and would blow up in the early 1990s grunge styles with flannel shirts, jeans, and baby doll dresses. The stability of one fashion item within the scene ebbs and flows, but overall Dr. Martens boots maintained some placement in many key subgenres and eras of punk style (AirWair Limited 1999).

A quick change of shoe and related accessories can transform a look into punk instantly. The appearance of an above-the-knee denim skirt worn to church can be transformed when opaque hosiery and flat loafers are replaced with fishnets and combat boots.

Controversial Representations

Dressing punk often means to appear contrarian. Coded cues are meant to differentiate the wearer from the crowd and to be understood by like-minded viewers. This is expressive and also distinctive from the context. A facial piercing may or may not be seen as obvious punk style depending on the context and possibly the demographics of the wearer. The same is true of a typically benign T-shirt, blue jeans, and athletic shoe ensemble that can be fashioned as punk with the addition of nonmainstream slogans and symbols.

This concept can also be bold and may result in offending a number of viewers. Text, picture, and body modification choices may invite discussion, debate, and even confrontation. These confrontational images worn in punk style reflect the challenge of a subcultural community built by those disenfranchised from the mainstream and highly critical of the norms that rejected their ideology. Examples of such imagery may include logos or patches supporting certain social causes, such as animal rights or freeing prisoners with controversial legal cases like Mumia Abu Jamal.

Punk's antiauthoritarian stance lends itself to some members opposing organized religion, and T-shirts emblazoned with "F*%! Christianity" were briefly popular in the 1990s. In punk style it is sometimes acceptable to use slogans and symbols on T-shirts and patches to admonish one belief system while it would be seen within punk as heinous to support the other side, even if that sort of boundary around speech is contrary to the individuality promoted within punk. Therefore since Christianity is the dominant religion in contemporary Western cultures, punks sometimes see a protest against that religion as part and parcel of antimainstream or antidogmatic thought. However, punks often do not wish to offend the underdog or cultures that are not dominant, as punks see themselves as separate from the mainstream in many ways, and consequently in current punk culture something such as a "F*%! Judaism" T-shirt would most likely be reviled as anti-Semitic. A debate exists inside the punk scene, and among its outside viewers, about the nature of wearing such grandstanding shirts, because punk, while subcultural, is a community unto itself and within it there are ideological trends.

Thus the exact root of these choices, and whether they exist in the framework of trend or ideology, can be blurry. This in part explains the brief period of time in the 1970s when some punks did in fact take to wearing swastikas. This was a sign of being very contrarian, and received mixed results at a time when irony was rarely used in clothing (McNeil and McCain 1996). Many punk wearers did not know the complete origins and lineage of the symbol with a 3,000-year history and used in many cultures. They solely associated it with its most nefarious use by the Nazi party (as most people reasonably do) (Roger, Interview with author, 2009).

This unlikely symbol was used in the early New York City punk scene, which had an abundance of Jewish individuals, including Richard Hell, Chris Stein from Blondie, and multiple Ramones. Some people of this scene were directly descended from Holocaust victims, yet wore the swastika as a form of punk aesthetic expression. As such, a link between the Holocaust and 1970s punks can be traced. It had an impact on Jewish punks and those from other backgrounds who were persecuted in World War II. It made some feel embarrassment for their ancestors who had been so victimized, and the displaying of a swastika was a way of standing up to oppressors using their own symbols comfortably and to be antagonistic, particularly in polite society. In this context Jewishness was perhaps equated with otherness, and the anti-Semitic sentiment can run deeper, particularly to people of Jewish heritage. Thus an embracing of that otherness, and appropriating the images of the labeler with satire and confrontational irony, was a core thread running through punk style, so it makes sense to have the Nazi symbol fall into this category (Beeber 2006).

Similar to the New York scene, in the 1970s the swastika became fairly popular among English punks and punk performers. Malcolm McLaren (who was Jewish) and those employed at SEX (the boutique he ran with Vivienne Westwood) used Nazi imagery regularly for a brief time. After the war it was occasionally worn by English bikers in the 1950s and 1960s. Stylist and designer Roger K. Burton, who is the founder of the Contemporary Wardrobe Collection, which is Europe's largest collection of street fashion, as well as the visual designer of Westwood and McLaren's "Worlds End" shop on Kings Road, explained:

> On the one hand it was rebellion, and on the other hand it was like … because don't forget, soldiers that fought in war, in [unintelligible] combat and stuff, would come back with souvenirs from the war. That German medal or knives with the swastika on some. You know, these things got handed out to their sons, who happened to be a biker, and they would wear the medal because you know, "My dad got this in the war." Like, stole it off some dead German or something. So there was a bit of that going on as well. (Interview with author, 2009)

Then 1970s punks took it on as a very shocking symbol that not all found tasteful. He further explained:

It's almost confusing … A bit of ironic-ness going on … Is it nostalgia, is it rebellion? … it's a bit of each, really … And all at the same time. And super hot button issue with people, obviously … But yeah, in this country it certainly did yeah; cause a few kind of alarm bells to ring as it were … Absolutely.

However not all punks found it tasteful, and when Siouxsie Sioux of the band Siouxsie and the Banshees donned the symbol, the band the Clash rejected it and would not allow Siouxsie to use its equipment at a shared music show. It did not dampen their relationship, but was a sign of rejection of a punk trend gone awry and crossing the fuzzy borders of what may be acceptable within punk style (Gray 2004). A punk wearing a swastika in the 1970s was particularly shocking as it went against the grain of where the political direction of punk was starting to head, although at the time many punks had not composed a complete political framework. However, with the right-wing National Front gaining steam in England and extolling sometimes open racism and violent confrontations, to left-wing groups it seemed naïve or hypocritical for a punk to wear a swastika solely to cause visual shock when there was so much going on to think about—things that were part of why punk was started as a movement (Gilmore 2011).

Of course, some use the swastika with less ironic sentiment, as there are always those who use the symbol purely as camp, abandoning morality and placing the design in unfamiliar contexts, and there are those who desire to align with dark forces no matter the naïveté they present. And there is a contingent within almost any group of people, including punks, who agree with the ideas of the Nazis or who resent things like wealth and education (sometimes as a component of what it is to be punk and antimainstream), therefore resulting in a sort of sympathizing with the symbolism the swastika came to represent about Jews or people perceived like them (Beeber 2006).

The rise of neo-Nazi skinheads attending punk shows did not gel well with the actual sentiments within punk initially because of the community's diverse makeup and later because of the bands' and music's heavily politicized, social justice overtones. Therefore a rejection of the use of the swastika and reactions against its wearers became inevitable.

The Origins of Punk Style

The initial basis of the visual style that would remain through today was formed in New York and London, with other geographic regions and subcultural branches proving fundamental to the evolution of the style as each manifestation added more layers. Punk grew to be international, but the generally agreed history is that the seeds of what would become the subculture were initially planted in Detroit and Ann Arbor, Michigan with the bands the MC5 and Iggy and the Stooges and the surrounding personalities. It then truly blossomed in New York City and London and was a product of the scenes local to those places as well as a reaction to those that preceded them. Cities such as Los Angeles, San Francisco, Boston, Washington, DC, Cleveland and Akron, Ohio, Minneapolis, and others around the globe have played large roles in adding new interpretations.

The ideology and stylistic components of punk had been building. The 1960s youth embraced an air of freedom as the hippies and civil rights movements gained momentum, making positive social changes and singing about it with flowers in their hair and love taking over the brain and groin. But the early to mid-1970s brought economic recession and political strife that created a darker mood for the youth in the urban centers of New York and London and college towns such as Ann Arbor, Michigan. This set the tone for punk to fester as the optimism and freedom of the previous generation was replaced with depression and anger. Furthermore, the enthusiastic counterculture of the 1960s, which revolutionized Western society, was now settling into the establishment and becoming more mundane (Polhemus 2010). Although this calming passivity was arising, social problems were of course still relevant with the next generation of youth poised to counter the dominant culture.

Throughout the 1970s, musical icons and youthful popular culture were styled with a certain brightness and lightness, exuding crisp cheer and extra effort, even when coming from the "natural" point of view left over from the hippies of the 1960s. Television's family-oriented Brady Bunch, decadent disco, the boyish Bay City Rollers, and the billowy singer-songwriter movement could all be viewed by punks as pretentious, overdone, exaggerated, and brimming with possible artifice.

David Bowie's otherworldly Ziggy Stardust and the glam rock movement were precursors to punk, filled with artifice but an intentional comment on beauty, sexuality, and out-casting that would be crucial facets of punk. Alice Cooper's snarling version of similar discontent was influential alongside other early heavy metal looks. In England, the barebones rock of the pub scene set a musical tone of stripped-down grit and aggression. Performances of the Rocky Horror Picture Show, which Westwood and McLaren costumed, featured proto-punk fashions merging sexy monsters and mayhem. The artwork of Genesis P-Orridge and Cosey Fanni Tutti displayed contrarian ideas that shocked viewers. These concepts very soon merged. Across the pond, Warhol collaborated with the Velvet Underground on subversive themes and sounds like nothing prior in popular music. Writer, DJ, and self-proclaimed groupie Cherry Vanilla was iconic for her flame-colored dyed hair, and the New York Dolls featured a gang of downtown rockers cross-dressed and vamped up, yet still gritty in presence. These forces would soon emerge under a new title that embraced all of it: punk.

The term *punk* developed out of a slang term used primarily against so-called delinquent youth and also in other situations of someone dominating another, such as in prison. In the 1970s, the word came to be associated with this new subculture through multiple routes, and the origins of the moniker are disputed. In 1975, New

York writer Legs McNeil started a magazine with friends John Holstrum and Ged Dunn by that name. In 1976, British journalist Caroline Coon labeled the Sex Pistols "punk" in an article (*Punk Britannia* 2012). Furthermore, members of the community seeking to take ownership of being disenfranchised and mocked flipped the term. In times of war, economic depression, and social injustice, the moniker "punk" claims a place in a society that while dissolving around punks still has the nerve to judge their antiauthority, contrarian counterculture lifestyle, dress, music, and attitude. Punk had become a point of pride indicating a refusal to give in, even latching on to outsider status (Leblanc 1999; Polhemus 2010).

Leblanc detailed this concept:

Early punks used inversion to create style, glorifying anything that connotated low status (dog collars), sexual perversion (bondage clothes), banality (fake leopard fur), or degeneracy (rubber clothes). In addition, punks subverted culturally valued objects connotating tradition (tartan kilt), conformity (the school jacket and tie), and authority (police and military trooper uniforms). (1999: 40)

While previous subcultures tried to affect a cool, upbeat, or elegant persona, even using a form of the punks was acknowledging the social distress around them, a subculture built at a time of economic crises and developed in eras when these punk generations constantly read how much worse off they are than their parents were (Polhemus 2010). Social critiques of the status quo are a foundation of punk and lead to its continued relevance because it is nonspecific in terms of era or demographic, but can be transformed to suit the context.

New York

In New York, the look came from the artists, bands, and individuals bubbling up from the street, and only moderately from the industry of designers, although they too were generally ingrained in the underground. Most punks at the time in New York were a cross between the dwindling hippie and glam movements, a low-budget street style, and a bit of art school panache. Gray explained:

None of the New York bands sounded alike, but what they had in common was a no frills approach to raw rock 'n' roll. Whether their hair was long or short, whether they wore ripped jeans and leather jackets and sneakers like The Ramones, or torn T-shirts and cheap sunglasses like Richard Hell, the style of the New York bands was similarly back-to-basics. (2004: 56)

The punk aesthetic synthesized motifs handed down from Warhol's Factory, pulp fiction, B movies, and comic books and infused with the economic pressures of a city on the brink of bankruptcy and young adults trying to grow into their own during such times (McKenna 1999; Polhemus 2010). A handful of individuals are often credited as the originators of what would become the New York punk look. However, many active players in the local scene contributed their take on downtown grunge and glamor. Individuals in fashion, music, retail, art, photography, and related fields all helped promote what would become punk style. Tish and Snooky's Manic Panic was the first store in the United States featuring punk wares. It opened in 1977 on St. Marks Place in NYC's East Village. Snooky says of that time:

Fig. 2.6 Tish and Snooky with storefront window display at Manic Panic, 1977 (copyright Manic Panic, photographer unknown).

People always loved our style, so we decided to try to sell it! Back then the neighborhood was really down and out—lots of empty storefronts, but the rent was really cheap. We sold our own original designs, as well as whatever else we liked—anything and everything punk: records, magazines, accessories, clothing, makeup and hair dye. Rockers like Johnny Thunders would put their clothes on consignment too! (Interview with author, 2012)

Richard Hell was another key innovator in the New York punk music community, and was known for being one of the first in that scene to don the short-haired, grungy, safety-pinned aesthetic, and McLaren would cite Hell as influential to the British look. However, a zeitgeist can leave behind an unclear history of originators, and often ideas burst forward simultaneously as they share influences. There is ongoing debate over the initial use of even some of the smallest details that are characteristic of punk. Roger said: "I think it just kind of happened. You know there's always the debate over who wore the first safety pin. It's like who fucking cares? It's a great idea, and somebody did it and everybody copied him" (Interview with author, 2009).

The Ramones made one of the biggest impacts. When the band performed at the CBGBs music venue in the mid-1970s, its members donned mostly black, favoring leather jackets, pegged pants, shaggy hair, and worn-through jeans and T-shirts. The image was a merger of antipopular fashion, street fashion, cartoon, and veneration of previous generations of youth. They were the antithesis of the shiny, bright, bell-bottomed look of the 1970s era. They did not appear polished or wealthy, but instead represented urban youth through their rebellious style and the forceful nature of their music (Rombes 2005: 14).

Johnny Thunders of the band the Heartbreakers, with his rock and roll persona and drug-addicted, but highly stylized appearance, also was a regularly referenced fashion template. His engineering boots and leather jackets were coveted items when seen by British fans. Marco said:

That whole motorcycle jacket thing came completely from New York. Because it's like when The Heartbreakers came out in late '76, because it was such a small scene of like really 50, 60 people, that suddenly like [Johnny] Thunders turns up in you know that black and white motorcycle jacket and [unintelligible] everyone had to have one. (Interview with author, 2009)

For women, there were multiple visual options, as exemplified by the lead singer of Blondie, Debbie Harry, with her effortless sex-kitten look, and by poet-musician Patti Smith with her androgynous, stripped-down Beat style; they could function in the same environment, with women of all stripes in between. Overall, the New York look was functional fashionable, overlaid with a gritty throwback Americana of denim and teen rebelliousness.

London

There was a great deal of cross-pollination of styles between New York and London as bands toured, counterculture communities mingled, and images spread through fanzines and records. Where New York punks were pop culture and the American dream turned on its head, British punks were cultural philosophy and art merged into a new style. The British punks looked to ideologies relevant in the era. Nihilism and Dadaism were influencing ideas, with founding members such as Malcolm McLaren and the manager of the Clash, Bernie Rhodes, seeking to emulate some of the principles of the Situationists and shift them into the rock world. A radical European art collective formed in the early 1950s, the Situationists were committed to pitching the world into a state of constant revolution and newness (McKenna 1999). World War II still hovered over the public consciousness in the 1970s as a heavy influence, hence the swastika usage and the blackout fabric some of the punk shirts were initially made from (Roger, Interview with author, 2009). The context was gritty, art driven, and heavy with social and political issues, and the clothes were a reaction to that surrounding. However a major stylistic difference in the United Kingdom was the root of the fashions, as they did not all originate from the street, but instead from core designers within yet also guiding the community. Marco said: "It didn't come from the street. It wasn't a street fashion. It wasn't a street fashion in the same way as skinhead or mod and Teddy Boy. It was created by two designers" (Interview with author, 2009).

Vivienne Westwood and Malcolm McLaren laid a foundation of stores featuring their designs on Kings Road that served as gathering spaces for like-minded souls to congregate. They created provocative styles featuring representations of bare breasts, naked men, passages of texts, and satirical images of the Queen, as well as rubber shirts, loose-knit mohair sweaters, and pieces with numerous straps and zippers simulating bondage attire. Westwood also developed the anarchy symbol in fashion of the capital A with the "no/anti-" slash through it ("T Screen Test Films" 2009). The images of sex, debated authority, and popular culture references were incredibly shocking at the time and tested the limits of freedom of artistic statement in public (Stolper and Wilson 2004). Some were even arrested for wearing the shirts, and authorities seized clothing from the stores and charged Malcolm McLaren with a version of indecent exhibition.

Notably outfitting the Sex Pistols, the designers also dressed the denizens who gathered, and those individuals would be empowered to promote their own creative innovations. A significant example is the key salesperson Jordan, whose eye-catching aesthetic pushed norms that still exist today. Similarly, a group of expressive young punks sometimes dubbed the Bromley Contingent,[4] who were active fans of the Sex Pistols and David Bowie before them, gained notoriety through media attention to their use of profanities on primetime television, their innovative bands, and raucous behavior. Featuring, among others, Siouxsie Sioux with her proto-goth styles, Soo Catwoman with her shaved head and pointed tufts of hair that resembled feline ears, Philip Salon who favored exaggerated costume-like styles, and Billy Idol with his bleached blonde leather rocker appearance, this group could not be missed, and many wanted to emulate its styles.

Westwood and McLaren's shop was not the only innovator of the British punk look: rocker Ian Dury was a style forerunner, wearing razor blade earrings and proto-punk attire, and other shops such as Acme Attractions and the stalls at Beaufort Market had their own products and followings. More designers, boutiques, and scenes of kids around the country were pertinent to punk's growth and increasing diversity, however the nucleus of what would become the caricature style was rooted in those early shops. Roger said: "Kings Road on a Saturday, you'd think there was a revolution going on. But anywhere else in the country … of course it spread, it was pretty small really, a few thousand people as opposed to hundreds of thousands."

Westwood and McLaren revamped and renamed their previous boutiques Let It Rock to Too Fast To Live Too Young To Die then to SEX and finally to Seditionaries. Where Let It Rock catered to the retro Teddy Boy subculture and other subcultures hanging on to the past, this new store spoke loudly about current issues and themes of the day and pushed boundaries of sexuality by selling fetish wear previously only available through mail order, as well as its own progressive designs (Polhemus 1994). In addition to trying to push contemporary buttons rather than recapturing old youth groups, they also sought to distance themselves from the racism and conservative nature of the Teds who frequented their earlier shops (Stolper and Wilson 2004). This would be slightly odd in light of the swastika emblem that made its way into punk fashion, but its sentiment generally served a different purpose. Also, it was not all heady and futuristic, as some of the distressed garments were inspired by the 1950s pulp pinup images Westwood and McLaren adored, which featured women looking washed ashore or even ravaged, with clothing ripped to shreds ("T Screen Test Films" 2009).

There were "be yourself" and "make a statement" elements that were impulsive and culturally aware, yet not overly self-reflexive. Marco said, "More just 'go, do, be' kind of a thing … what it looks like doesn't matter" (Interview with author, 2009). Polhemus describes how it continued to emerge in a highly diverse manner throughout 1976 and what was worn to music clubs such as the popular hangout Louise's:

A few wore fetishistic outfits in rubber or PVC—either from SEX or from the kinky "glamourwear" firm She 'N' Me. Some wore deliberately battered school blazers with loose and dangling ties. Some wore see-through string vests or combinations of army surplus and cheap lingerie. There were a lot of leather jackets and some early experiments with "tribal" hair and makeup. And yes, there were a few kids wearing the binliners, Dr. Martens boots, ripped T-shirts, dog-collars, safety pins and tight drainpipes which would become the media's Punk stereotype. But many flaunted the "dressy" attire that would later be associated with the New Romantics. (1994: 92)

All of these elements swirled together to compose punk style. As Westwood's profile grew, bands toured, and the scene on both continents gained media exposure, those involved in the regional communities got to know one another, and many new individuals found their calling and joined the ranks. Visual particulars started to be signifiers of kinship and inclusion, even if it meant some loss of the original intent of individuality and rebellion against conformity.

From New York to London, and the global takeover that came, punk style continued to reinvent itself regularly, and through the years that followed it visually built on the aesthetic platform, creating a spectrum of styles. A merging of the New York and London looks went on to influence and be influenced by the deconstructionist high fashion of the early 1980s, specifically out of Japan, the skate and surf fashions of the California coast, and subsequent subcultures, many of which would be folded into the punk bosom. In-the-scene photographers would capture images of punks from the stage to their bedrooms, ranging from icons to individuals who would disappear into obscurity. These photos have a lasting effect on future generations of subcultural participants who look to the past for their ideas of punk dress.

Precedents and Influencers of Punk Style

The level of shock and use of irony in punk attire felt fresh, however not everything about the style was entirely new. Punks admired certain subcultures predating their own, and traced their feelings of counterculture, antiauthority, DIY, and other contrarian beliefs to some who came before them, particularly those appropriating conventional forms of daily life into social commentary. Within and outside of subculture much of dress has been politicized and demonstrated social relevance. At the time, these contemporary British rebels, using their own creativity, their environments, and their influences helped shape what the punk look would be. Punk style is representative of the ideas of the time, even if the time is fluid and continuous because punk has lasted decades, just as previous styles have come out of their countercultures and avant-garde communities. All of that contributed to what would become the punk lifestyle and aesthetic.

Earlier countercultures set the path for punk style to follow in their footsteps. It can be seen in the beatniks' black attire, the haircuts from the rockabillys, teds, and greasers, slim-cut suits from the mods, cropped hair and tight jeans from the skins, and military attire from the hippies. Punk as a movement was shaped in part by the development of philosophies dedicated to youth, jazz, rhythm and blues, and rock and roll, as well as corresponding components such as car and bike enthusiasts and literary scenes. Rebellious anticonformists such as political, philosophical, and cultural protesters have been influential in punk styles. The punk ideology has traveled similar roads, and thus the dress and aesthetic cues reflects those paths. Early twentieth-century movements like the Lettrists and the Situationists and mid-century movements such as the hippies (who punks detested but did gather some influence from), and the women's rights and gay rights movements of the 1970s all wore their politics on their sleeve, often literally with strong visual identifiers. Writing statements on oneself and clothing, wearing military jackets as an ironic statement, were greatly used in punk dress for fashion purposes and to continue the statement beyond the protest and into daily life. This can be seen in the DIY style of lettering, such as the ransom note style seen in designer Jamie Reid's Sex Pistols logo. Urban graffiti left its mark on punk style as an art form, typography, and social statement about property and public expression. When a garment is adorned with strong sentiments in text or design, it is useful that they can be read from near and far and that the viewer is enraptured by the visual volume. There is great power for the wearer when the viewer is rendered unable to escape the conversation, even if it's only briefly in their own head, such as when a T-shirt has controversial images on it (Marcus 1990).

Artistic and fashion movements also influenced punk style. Dadaists, dedicated to opposing the aesthetic and social values of their time, morphed into surrealism, and among the sentiments shared by these far-flung conspirators was a disdain for the mannered perversions of high art (McKenna 1999). They had a goal to shock and to smack in the face things of "good taste." They used to make statements in addition to self-expression and sounded alarms on popular culture, consumerism, and mainstream lifestyles, drew attention to the frivolity and banality of some of it, and heralded the mundane as special. Artists that closely predated punk, from Warhol with his soup cans and mass duplication to Duchamp with his toilet, showed the mundane could be turned on its head and transformed into art and commentary with a strong dose of humor. The Surrealists and related designers, such as Schiaparelli with her lobster hats (now seen on Lady Gaga by way of Isabella Blow/Philip Treacy) gave the world an avant-garde zest that influenced punk's take on dress. Schiaparelli also used nonfunctional zippers as ornamentation, which Westwood later popularized. New textiles such as synthetic fabrics developed during World War II, as well as artistic methods such as silk screening, revolutionized art and added the ability to create multiples quickly, accurately, and affordably. The accessible format of silk screening would especially provide the chance to quickly signify changing interests in certain punk bands, political sentiments, or attendance at events. Fashion progressions such as the shifting of women into pants and reducing the volume of structure undergarments adjusted the silhouette and the cultural symbolism of the design.

The craft movement continued to ebb and flow throughout the late 1800s to its rebirth in the twenty-first century, influencing subcultures and taking in influences from them. DIY provides satisfaction by promoting individuality and personalization through self-reliance outside of the consumer system. There is also an empowering notion from the ability to create something oneself. This approach provides room for personalization of politics whether it is slogan or shape or fabric. Mid-century pioneers in modern design were another forerunner to DIY within punk. Charles and Ray Eames and Russell Wright brought affordable and functional design into the mainstream and took the beauty of art and incorporated it into mundane things. Originally those designs were conceived as a democratization of design accessibility where advancements in form and function could be aligned with everyone. Punk fashion continues to be influenced by design movements, as the high-tech era would usher in cyberpunk styles where the merger of technology and edgy aesthetics would bring circuitry and lighted accents to punk-themed attire.

The various countercultural, political, artistic, and design movements that predated punk all helped shape its vision of improving on the everyday through continued social critique, increasing accessibility, and adding an interesting flair to the otherwise mundane.

Where It Would Go: Diversity and the Development of Subgenres

The iconic look of plaid bondage pants, a mohawk, and ripped band T-shirt is partially based on the appearance of the punk scene's original musical, social, and stylistic leaders. Over time new generations discovered and reinterpreted those initial influences for themselves, understood the connection the style leaders of the early punk scene made between, say, rockabilly and punk, and then were influenced by both simultaneously. Examples include a contemporary punk who is also into skinhead, mod, or skateboard culture. New generations also have dealt with their own sociopolitical issues that they visually incorporate into new variations of dress.

The late 1970s to the present saw some of the classic punk styles become static and new images incorporated. These fresh representations of a punk lifestyle were motivated by changing geographic hubs, varying activities associated with each subscene, and the cross-cultural influence of trends outside of punk. These forces would refresh the visuals through the use of vintage clothes including pin-up and garage styles (which harkens back to some of Westwood's earliest influences); Los Angeles-oriented surf and skateboard attire including baggy pants and colored slip-on canvas shoes; sportswear including oversized sweatshirts and white thick-soled athletic shoes; and aesthetic influences from parallel subcultures such as goth's dark drama and hip-hop's urban influence.

Nora explained there are many routes to meeting the basic aesthetic and thematic goals:

> It splinters off into everything from the vintage rockabilly set to the, the strappy bondage pants, mall punk, to the genuine gutter punks that own four shirts and keep them until they're falling off of them. Squatter style. And then there's the goth kids. So there's all these different subcultural visuals that pop into my head, kind of like a family tree I suppose. But ... I'm definitely not a believer that there's a uniform or that there's a measurable this is and this isn't. I think a lot of it is how you wear it too.

Punk always had a diverse population folding in individual ideas about style, and this became magnified as time went on. It could be said to have started with the fact that original punks were an ethnically, racially, and economically diverse group. Marco noted: "there was no great decision about what 'this' is. It was just a bunch of people doing what they were doing. No one ever said, 'it's this. And we're doing this today,' you know, 'And we stand for this.' It was just … people who had the same general point of view gathering" (Interview with author, 2009). There has always been a large middle-class population within punk, and the diversity within punk has always been brought together by criticism of the status quo, including disdain for previous subcultures (in the proto-punks' case, the hippies) who they felt let down the cause and were becoming part of the establishment (Polhemus 2010). A great deal of punk as it would continue in the 1980s, 1990s, and 2000s was based in middle-class culture, including the college educated, and this informed the tone of the political activism. It is a stereotype that all punk is "gutter punk" and even among those not all people who are blatantly poor; however, some are saddled in other ways such as student debt or situated in downtrodden economies that mean their generations are worse off than those previous—a depressing state that causes judgment of the system.

Individual punks create their own personalization on the style based on their experiences. Furthermore, subgroups of punks may collectively develop a style appropriate to the particulars of their context and concepts. Therefore each subgenre has detailed corresponding visual characteristics that meet the needs of that scene as well as follow the catalyst of pioneering community leaders. They are all branches of a large family tree with limbs going in numerous directions yet with intertwined roots. The like-minded and those with similar backgrounds and interests linked together to form subgroups cemented by their take on punk ideology. These subgroups then developed their own angles on punk style, utilizing some of the initial characteristics shaped within the New York and London scenes, but that were also regionally specific and innovated by leaders within each new community.

While the elaborate British style became the go-to stereotype, it was in fact the New York style—casual with subtle artistic flair—that permeated much of where international punk style would progress, having been adopted by skateboarders, hardcore kids, emo fans, and other subcultural factions that developed. This is not to say the British iconic look only exists in cartoon forms, or that it does not have a place in modern punk culture. There are certainly still numerous punks adorned in that manner, and aesthetic elements of it remain vital. However the head-to-toe iconic ensemble is a rarity on any given street and even at a punk event. Yet more subtle versions of what punk style has become are in fact everywhere, inspired by original punk styles and reflecting that individual's punk experience in his or her region and time period.

From the late 1970s into the 1980s, California was where the New York grit and London flamboyance thematically mixed, as well as being a hotbed for its own colorful creativity. Los Angeles took part in heading the transition to new types of punk styles as they would be influenced by the Day-Glo and performance orientation of London merged with skate and surf attire, yet also had their own brand of hard-hitting punk with bands such as Black Flag and the Circle Jerks, many of whose members wore jeans and T-shirts. The Bay Area developed into a central location for punk scenes related to ska music, bringing in those styles and a heavy dose of sociocultural politics using influence from various British scenes' blatant statement pieces. By the 1990s, San Diego played a role in another retooling with polished styles that emphasized crisp and trim looks. Because of the sizeable scenes in California with a strong infrastructure for disseminating ideas, these looks traveled across the country and the world.

However the volume of punk styles coming out of California was not alone. As new scenes developed en masse, those with the most substantive records or personalities often transferred their visual and material inspirations onto their kin. Often the name of the punk subgenre that arose gives a clue into its related aesthetic. Numerous small groups within each subgenre take on their own nickname, musical style, and fashions. While the evolution keeps going and the niche areas are nearly unlimited, the following sections examine some of the more prominent subgenres to emerge.

Hardcore

The development of the hardcore subgenre is a point when punk style took a detour from the iconic style. Specifics were shaped through regional and personality influences, and scenes developed styles that spoke to their experiences and to the priorities of this subgenre that explored some of the same, yet different concepts than the initial punk movement. There have always been people for whom the iconic punk style felt overblown or like a costume, rather than an artistic expression of difference. For them standard daily wear could easily merge with spirited punk music and lifestyles (Pappalardo 2012). With this, hardcore took influence from athletic gear, mainstream sportswear, skinhead attire, blue-collar work, and the military with a few divergent outcomes. The look of hardcore was more accessible regarding a conventional Western framework of dress concepts, yet also more masculine than the early punk dress (Leblanc 1999), thus in some ways less inclusive of the wide spectrum of diverse people who initially embraced punk. Hardcore's streamlined appearance stepped away from the use of bright colors, elaborate hair, cosmetics, and accessories and primarily featured attire accepted within the norm yet imbued with cues to its subcultural affiliation. Shaved heads, athletic jerseys, tattoos, and woven cotton pants by brands such as Dickies grew into a norm (Blush 2001).

Images of Washington, DC bands from the 1980s and 1990s, such as Minor Threat, were pivotal in the transition to a more subtle style, as the band members appeared like

Fig. 2.7 Punk style including aesthetic influences from skinheads and overlapping with hardcore and iconic punk elements, Wycombe UK, 1980s (copyright PYMCA, photographer Gavin Watson).

they could have been anyone in the suburban United States, dressed covertly punk in sweatshirts, shorts, athletic shoes, and T-shirts, stripping away the elaborate dress of earlier scenes (Nedorostek and Pappalardo 2008). As preppy and power dressing came into vogue in that era, the dressed-down punks created a countertrend. The DC style of short, natural hair, work pants, skateboard shoes or boots, small knit caps, and dark T-shirts became a signature punk aesthetic.

The Boston scene brought influences of the regional culture and the chilly weather. Jeans, hoodies, leather jackets, and boots were the dominant styles. Details such as the self-removal of shirtsleeves created tops with increased mobility to allow one to enthusiastically move one's whole body along with the music at the shows. As a matter of logical function, the sleeves were not always discarded and sometimes were used as a head covering, particularly as the nip of cold air could be felt against a bald shave (Nedorostek and Pappalardo 2008).

New York's early hardcore style was influenced in part by the skinhead style associated with the band Agnostic Front. It shifted to reflect suburban types of clothing preferred in neighboring Connecticut with varsity jackets and Champion brand sweatshirts as worn by fans of the band Youth of Today (Nedorostek and Pappalardo 2008; Brian Peterson, Interview with author, 2011). Variations on this athletic style were favored by many suburban kids and featured often in "youth crew" groupings. Numerous subgroups had their own take on the style, generally citing a preferred word then the suffix "-core," such as horror-core or krishna-core, with music and dress details that reflected what the name implies.

Brian Peterson, author of the book *Burning Front* about the history of the 1990s hardcore scene, said:

> By the mid-90s it was often all about baggier clothes. Tattoos and piercings also became more popular, though not as popular as they became in the 00s ... By the later 90s, some people were wearing super tight clothing, which some felt was influenced by the look of some of the bands from the San Diego punk/hardcore scene. The Midwest was always a mish-mash of everything. (Interview with author, 2011)

The emergence of hardcore style created a rift within the punk scene regarding who was exemplifying punk ideology most accurately through fashion, music, and behavior. Some would argue that hardcore was a separate subculture from punk. Initially this debate was fairly severe, however it has somewhat diffused over time through the natural progression of styles overlapping and continuing to evolve.

Emo and Indie

Emo, derived from the word emotional, and indie, short for independent (of major record labels, but also perhaps of mainstream trappings), were sibling subgenres of punk with roots in hardcore as well as the music culture that permeated college radio stations and MTV's 120 Minutes and Alternative Nation programs in the 1980s and 1990s. They can be discussed in unison here for some of their overlapping characteristics, although they do differ in some areas.

Both utilized, but softened, the athletic and utilitarian aspects of hardcore in music and in fashion, shifting toward a retro, collegiate, and skateboard emphasis, with some goth overtones in the 2000s. "Emo" and "indie punks" would adopt descriptive names such as "sweater punks,"[5] "math rocker,"[6] and "Romulans,"[7] in reflection of their scholarly, detailed appearance generated to reflect the detailed layers in the output of their material, be it zines, complicated song structures, or coded love songs. These fact these subgenres were co-ed also influenced the dress, and trends navigated the manner of the style through periods of asexual skinny black attire to unisexual baggy

T-shirts and jeans to hyper-gender accentuated retro dresses and rocker chic. These looks of white belts, trim black T-shirts, and neatly coiffed hair and perfectly chosen cardigan sweaters were a few of the versions that alluded to a reaction against both the spontaneous hodgepodge of the iconic punk style and the sporty hardcore affect (Nedorostek and Pappalardo 2008). Emo and its related scenes also took on heavy sociopolitical overtones; the attire was very reflective of this and often cruelty free (no fur, no leather). Backpacks filled with zines, stickers, and the like were the norm.

Riot Grrrl

In the 1980s, much of the punk subculture shifted toward hardcore and away from some of its initial gender balance, and the attire grew to reflect its predominantly male inhabitants. Other musical and artistic countercultures emerged, more openly embracing femininity, homosexuality, and variations on male representations. Thus the women in the punk scene reflected an appearance that generally did not empha-size Western traditional female gender roles and aesthetics. This would sometimes manifest in styles such as a shaved head with bangs or a tuft up front, big boots, and plaid skirts (Blush 2001).

In the 1990s, the Riot Grrrl movement attempted to re-highlight the female ex-perience and female sexuality, trying to skew it back to influences offered from the earlier waves of punks (Marcus 2010). Riot Grrrls were third-wave feminists who comprised a collective movement with both centralized geographics and leaders, and decentralization as it was very regional as well. They consciously exagger-ated their femininity in satirical and ironic ways, and embraced womanhood and girlhood. Hyper-feminine baby doll dresses and form-fitting T-shirts, accessorized with uber-intellectual retro eyeglasses and combined with the potent aggression of combat boots, expressed conflicting messages of the complexity of their experience. They made protest signs of their bodies through words and phrases inscribed with Sharpie ink on arms and stomachs. This method was a way to broadcast a message, draw attention to their sentiments, and identify one another (Marcus 2010).

Sara Marcus, author of *Girls to the Front* about the history of the Riot Grrrl move-ment, said:

> Olympia girls talked about the fact that many of them cut their bangs short, dyed their hair bright colors, and wore thrift-store dresses and cardigans. DC punk scene was typi-cally more androgynous—cargo shorts, band T-shirts—and even though the Olympia musicians who lived there in the summer of 1991 stood out for their more feminine style, DC Riot Grrrl style overall tended to be more in line with the city's punk style overall, with the addition of little-girl barrettes. (Interview with author, 2011)

Their aesthetic was influenced visually by childhood attire, the weather and cul-ture in the Pacific Northwest and Washington, DC (regions where the movement blossomed), and college experiences—a style that reflected pride in education and knowing-ness, such as vintage dresses with an awareness of their history and glasses that embraced a bookish look. Leblanc (1999) explained that female punks have often found sartorial creativity in inviting contrast between mainstream feminine styles with punk visual cues in one ensemble.

Anarcho and Crusty

A subset of punks who are frequently anarchists, reside communally and/or on the streets, and often travel by train hopping are known as crust or crusty, gutter, d-beat, and anarcho punks. There are also some punks with an affinity for these styles yet who do not necessarily exact all aspects of the lifestyle; they do, however, maintain some of the aesthetics to represent the spirit associated with the style. They mix the iconic UK punk styles with a biker toughness and the nomadic, unwashed appearance often reflective of their living in squats. The colors are frequently dark, and the attire is often utilitarian such as cargo pants, denim, and T-shirts, and has frequently been self-manipulated by cutting the shirt to have no sleeves or adding embellishments including patches of favorite bands. Accessories and body modifications may include dreadlocks, piercings, and tattoos, with flaps of fabric covering their behinds often adorned with band names or anarchist symbols with the practical implications of keeping dry when sitting on a curb (Blush 2001).

Skatepunk

By the 1990s, hardcore, emo, and indie overlapped heavily with the interests of surf and skate culture and skatepunk emerged as an integrated offshoot. Named for their favorite lifestyle/hobby, frequently male (although not always), they wore garments useful for their pastime such as loose-fitting pants, Vans shoes, baseball caps, snow hats, and T-shirts. Not all skaters were punks, as there was also quite a bit of crossover with hip-hop, electronic music, and other subcultures, and the intermingling within skate culture had enormous bearing on the aesthetic. Their casual appearance was slightly unkempt, and the look was masculine yet not overtly combative, although still athletic and aggressive, matching the extreme nature of the sport when at its best. Videos and magazines featured acclaimed skaters as well as tours of demonstrations and competitions, spreading skateboard tricks and dress styles.

Brian Peterson commented:

> In the '90s, hardcore was a mix of a lot that was going on in other aspects of culture and art. For instance, the baggier look was popular in skating, underground hip-hop, and

Fig. 2.8 Skateboarder style (copyright Getty, photographer Lisa Pines, collection Photodisc).

raver culture. I saw a lot of commonalities among these types of groups at that point, and it is only natural that style would be one of them. (Interview with author, 2011)

While his example was about the effect of blending on hardcore, his sentiment could carry over to many forms within punk, including what happened with skate-punks specifically.

Cyberpunk/Steampunk

Cyberpunk is a science fiction genre that developed a dress style to reflect its themes, often regarding the individual as marginalized or isolated within a dystopic future that includes vast technological innovations, sometimes to the point of invasiveness in body and spirit. The resulting aesthetic merges a punk look with influences from films such as *Blade Runner,* as well as the goth, psychedelic, and dance scenes. The style also features the use of the color black with brights, including electronic lights and reflectors and metal pieces as trim, as well as a wide mix of proportions such as small tops with vastly oversized bottoms or platform shoes. Obvious nods to technology may come in circuitry or tubing as trim on garments.

Steampunk is an adaptation of cyberpunk in its use of alternate scientific reality; however, instead of the future, it is focused on eras that closely predated the Industrial Revolution and electricity, such as the Wild West and the Edwardian and Victorian times. In these settings it is imagined that steam was the primary power used, and often there is an emphasis on imagined innovations that may have been conceived in lieu of those that currently exist, as well as those that are no longer popular such as airships and analog computing. The dress styles are developed out of this merger of known clothing from historical periods, creatively mixed hypothesized visualizations of the attire that would match the imagined technology and resulting culture. Design and function are greatly interrelated, and often garments or accessories can be multitasked as tools. Using punk attire as a core, the colors worn may include blacks, grays, browns, and copper, with burnished metal accents and structured layers for both men and women; films such as *The Time Machine* and *20,000 Leagues Under the Sea* help set the tone.

Conclusions

Punk dress cannot be quantified or boiled down to an exact definition. The lasting physical styles include general aesthetic parameters like chunky, black, and silver, and specific garments such as boots, fishnets, and T-shirts. Although form is important, overall themes describing punk dress were often culturally or motivationally oriented related to attitude, time commitment, and differentiation from others.

Punk style is a mix of individual creativity, the artistic visions of designers, and cultural contexts shaping functional and social dress. There is debate about who created what when, as many try to claim originator status. Designer Zandra Rhodes, who was creating fashions with deconstruction and a form of the punk look in the 1970s, discussed how the kids on the street were innovating new styles: "I think it was definitely something that happened really from the streets by kids that could do their own couture without having to be able to afford it" (Interview with author, 2009). However, Marco feels the true punk looks came from designers, whose styles were communicated to the young by the media. "I hated all this kind of let's do it yourself kind of [attitude] ... I don't understand who told you this. [In] the beginning of '77, the papers picked up on it. They thought, 'Oh, this is shocking. This is some swearing in here ... We could sell some tabloids on it'" (Interview with author,

2009). The year 1977 became cited in shorthand to reference elaborately dressed punks. With that media and previously outsider attention, Marco feels designer looks influenced the kids on the street who wanted to replicate punk's aggression and rebellion.

Many punks initially mixed and matched street and designer, but often did not create the clothes themselves from scratch (Polhemus 2010). People have always dressed punk in a combination of actually making things from scratch, as well as styling themselves using ready-made items, so it is not always a craft project, but the craft is in the styling. Very few made their clothes, but many embellished them. With the recent modern craft movement has come an uptick in DIY in making all items, although even with that it is mostly accessories. All is satisfying as long as the result is eye catching and distinctive.

Nora explains that, although there are different categories within punk, there are no firm lines between the categories or strictly enforced rules about the styles:

> The first thing for me and I think for a lot of other people is it is definitely something that makes people look twice. And that goes for whether it is Japanese street style or American gutter punk or skinhead style. Anything that sticks out enough that people will actually stop and try to figure out what they're seeing.

Some would feel challenged when they dressed in a more refined manner or less blatantly than the iconic punk style. Yet this is a way in which punk continues to evolve and remain fresh. Punks often incorporate common popular youth/main-stream/high fashion contemporary style for the era with a reaction to it either through subtle changes in the form or the use of the object in context. There is also often a hearty dose of tribute to the lineage of the scene that would challenge their invest-ment in the subculture (Blush 2001; Sklar 2010). A variety of appearances became accepted within the scene as punk styles, and were recognized as punk by outsiders.

A significant theme is that there is often a difference between how punks define the physicality of iconic punk dress, rooted in the 1970s British styles, and how they actually wear punk attire. This is for various reasons. They are much more focused on motivations, perception, expression, and attitude than on staying true to a uni-form. Punks are potentially more flexible when it comes to dress for nonpunk con-texts than an outsider may believe. Also, even though their outward punk appearance may not be stereotypically representative, they may be more committed to punk than an outsider may realize, as subtle punk cues are covertly employed. A lot of what punk dress is today is heavily coded and subtle, while harkening back to the iconic pieces of its history. It is progressive yet retains a heritage.

Globalization and the Internet era have brought increased cross-pollination be-tween cultures, including different forms of fashion. In punk many more subgroups emerged, often developing layers within layers, each with its own variation on the core punk styles; reflective of their new concepts and subgenre members harkening back to the past in blatant or subtle ways. Within each time period, geographic region, particular scene, and among individuals it is worked out whether the branches interact or are distinct, and how much they influence each other in terms of style. There has also developed quite a bit of overlapping between styles; what is considered punk is now an amalgamation of all of those things. Some debate what qualifies under the parameters they interpret as legitimate to the title, however the debate itself indicates there is a postmodern multiplicity to punk style.

All of the influences have merged together, combined with the diversity of people within punk. Thus a blend of postmodern hodge-podge creates all that is punk style under one umbrella. Time would see punk morph and splinter with a variety of styles acceptable under the punk umbrella, which has been influenced by numerous concepts. Many take punk "spirit" and pick and choose visual signifiers to latch on to and make "punk" blended with modern time. Denise said:

> My experience and all of my friends and the people that I hang out with and see it's a lot of T-shirts. A lot of jeans or cut-off shorts … nothing necessarily clean and straight lines and form-fitting per se … casual and comfortable and chunky. Lots of boots, lots of big jewelry, lots of heavy kinds of things. Metals and things like that, silvery.

Denise's style represents where a lot of punks are at now, merging influences from the flashy London to the easy to the gritty New York to the athletic and work wear of hardcore and its related subgenres.

Within and outside of subculture, much of dress has been politicized and demonstrates social relevance. Punk style, especially in the United Kingdom, was very self-conscious and part art project, part design, part political and class revolution, rebelling against working-class drudgery and often filled with humor (Gilmore 1998). The goal was to put ideas on display like a canvas for shock, critique, or discussion. For punks in the United States, the inspiration for the style was art mixed with a more utilitarian goal of being functionally wearable and comfortable, and the rebellion may have been more against the rich and the boredom and social constraints of suburban life (Gilmore 1998).

Snooky elaborated:

> The UK and the US punk styles were different from each other. In the UK the look was more extreme and clearly defined. In the US it was more a mix of punk and '50's and '60's retro. The common denominator was rebellion against the status quo—against corporate rock, big record companies and boring fashion. The spirit was totally DIY; from the clothing to the hair to the music. The styles reflected the music … The point of the style was to clash against the contemporary styles of the time. It wasn't fashion but the complete opposite—it was anti-fashion.

While the tenets of this community were not 100 percent brand new concepts, the subculture that took on the name *punk* was louder and more confrontational than many of its predecessors. Also, while there were successful designers, musicians, and wealthy people in the scene, one of the major tenets of punk is its accessibility. Among punk there always were and still are youthful cliques with defined insiders and outsiders, however conceptually punk was built and continues to grow on the notion of its umbrella coverage of subcultural movements and universal acceptance of many types of social critique and of people who are not mainstream.

Punk style today incorporates the varied perspectives brought into its fold over time. The early punks were mostly youth, so punk style needed to change to suit these people growing up as well as to suit the next wave of youth coming into the fold. It is malleable in that way. Unlike the hippies, who primarily abandoned their style with adulthood as it mostly remained stuck in time, punk is more akin to hip-hop where there are adult versions and different versions to suit its changing community and maturing individuals.

Punk Style Motivations and Explanations

When I was eighteen, I got my eyebrow pierced with a chunky silver barbell. I went to a local piercing studio with some friends from punk bands who were already experienced in this respect. While not my first or last punk-style body modification, this remains the grand stand-off piercing as it was in my face for all to see, not occasionally covered by hair or clothes, but a blatant statement.

It was a bit of an ordeal to get, as the first try did not work out and had to be redone. Piercing barbells consist of a straight bar with balls on each side; one of the balls unscrews to allow the wearer to slip the metal rod through a piercing. The rod is placed in a hollow needle and plunged through the skin; the loose ball is screwed back into place. The problem I faced was that, instead of the rod slipping out of the needle nicely, it was stuck as the needle used was a bit too small. I saw the blood drain from my friends' faces and they tried to convince me it was no big deal. The piercer could not remove the barbell from the needle, therefore the whole thing had to come back through the skin and a new barbell placed in an appropriately sized needle. Fifteen years later, I replaced it with a slightly smaller silver barbell to maintain the same appearance, only moderately more refined. It took me that long to do the replacement as my fumbled process left me a bit unnerved.

Years prior to the eyebrow piercing, I was one of the first people I know to have the upper cartilage of the ear pierced, and then much of the rest of my ear was also adorned with small hoops. After the eyebrow piercing I had the piercings in my lobes stretched to wider openings and I wore specific jewelry constructed for these larger-sized holes. These piercings were performed everywhere from jewelry stores in shopping malls to punk houses while bands played in basements below to acclaimed piercing studios.[1] Over the years some of the holes became infected and closed up, some I lost interest in and abandoned, and some I alternated between attention-getting jewelry and subtle or even obscured choices.

But the facial piercing has stayed and for various reasons means more to me than the rest. It still speaks volumes, but also has become an almost understated part of who I am and what I look like. It is apparent in every photo taken of me, from those at rock shows to my wedding day. I have had family members tell me they do not even see it anymore and others say they cannot imagine me without it. It continues to play a role in my hiring process for employment, and has socially aligned me with crowds I do not call my own. Overall, I like the aesthetic, and I find comfort knowing that it links me to subculture and challenges Western beauty standards. I enjoy the thought process it provides for others when dealing with me. For some it is a sign of kinship, for others an indication I may be aggressive or contrarian or unintelligent, while for others it means very little at all.

Numerous cultures use modifications on the face, such as the Hindu bindi or the orthodox Jewish beard, as rites of passage and markers of demographic placement. They are visual representations of an ideological belief system. When you mix the facial piercing with other factors of my demographics that I visually present including education and lifestyle choices, it all comes together to form my entire identity. Although not too radical an item, quite a bit of identity salience is presented in one little piece of metal, less than an inch big, but that happens to be placed in my waxed and sculpted eyebrows.

Why a Person Might Choose Punk Styles

There is no simple way to answer the question "why does someone dress in a punk style?" Motivations cannot be entirely quantified, however there are dominant themes that drive many to make stylistic choices toward a punk look. Punk style is a way to express individual identity, as it addresses internal emotions as well as lifestyle choices and position within society. The individual choosing punk dress may be expressing internal feelings as well as trying to find external recognition for his or her expressions generating recognition that he or she is punk and causing the proper reactions such as distance or closeness among viewers.

For some, employing a blatant punk style is a strong method to express a punk ideology or salient punk identity. For others, utilizing the dress choices associated with punk is seen as an afterthought or perhaps something they do not consider relevant to their punk identity. A third group wears what appears to be punk style but does not align with the punk community or feel it has a salient punk identity.

Punks identify with broad concepts to fully explain punk dress. Certain style markers have become identifiable as punk, whether visible cues used by insiders, or demonstrations of a caricature by outsiders, or simply trend items from time to time in the fashion cycle. These stylistic characteristics become the cultural hallmarks of what makes dress practices *punk*. These markers developed over time and continue to evolve and diversify. In many ways, the cultural hallmarks bear a stronger weight to identify punk dress than the specifics of form, even though to an outside viewer the form is the dominant way to quickly attempt to note who is dressed in punk attire and therefore could be identified as punk. The visual and form is important, however the cultural hallmarks underscore everything and create the framework the style represents.

Punk dress is not always aligned with specific garments, as sometimes any garment can be presented as punk when the wearer is punk. Rachel explained, "I think it has more to do with attitude than it does with what you actually have on your body." Punks use words such as *mentality* and *attitude* to describe this. Brake (1985) referred to this as *argot,* meaning that one successfully embodies clothes with an attitude someone else might look uncomfortable in, or not seem appropriate wearing if they fail to have the heart in it.

Zhac added:

> I'm older … So when I was a punk rocker, a lot of it was about attitude. It wasn't so much the clothing. We didn't have Hot Topic, you know. There wasn't anybody that was catering to a punk aesthetic like there is now … You know, it was a lot more, reflected personality a lot more I think back then.

Punk style wrestles with its position with the mainstream, in part because of the challenge of how to outwardly represent a punk identity. There is a simultaneous goal to be separate yet accepted; a wish to relate to the mainstream enough to be perceived as appropriate within a certain context yet not have punk style appropriated by people who are not punk. There is a goal to influence culture but also to be insular and oriented toward secret symbolic cues learned through commitment. Examples include knowing band names, references, inside jokes, or, even better, band logos and images with no text. Some of these notions are conflicting and create internal battles such as how to dress punk in a nonpunk environment. Yet many of these ideas can exist through overlapping aesthetics and different individuals highlighting different priorities. Some, however, would argue this can lead to a certain amount of hypocrisy when trying to embed so many ideas within one's appearance.

Expression of Identity

A strategic use of dress aims to achieve certain goals for the wearer. However, the manner in which people express their identities using dress is complex. Roach-Higgins and Eicher (1992) theorized that dress is of great importance in communicating an identity. Dress seeks to achieve goals such as gaining respect, showing community involvement, or displaying sexuality. Identity is a merger of things one aligns with, roles one is enacting, and internal feelings about the self.

Identity theory refers to an individual's composite self that includes the multiple identities tied to social roles an individual plays (Goffman 1959; James 1890; Mead 1934). One's social roles often have a way of expressing outwardly, with meanings and ideas connected to one's external presence, which the individual internalizes and develops as a personal identity (Goffman 1959; Stone 1962; Stryker 1980; Stryker and Burke 2000). Dress plays a large, although at times complicated, part in the identity expression of an individual coming into his or her own in a certain role (Roach-Higgins and Eicher 1992). Meanings and ideas regarding an external role, such as a

Fig. 3.1 Casual style with DIY embellishments (copyright P. Kime Le).

job, are internalized as a role identity within an individual's self. Often dress is part of an individual coming into his or her own in a certain role.

A second reason to express a punk identity is to assert one of multiple identities within the same person. If a person has more than one aspect of himself he considers important parts of his identity, he might choose to express the punk part of his identity because it is the most salient (James 1890; Mead 1934; Stryker and Burke 2000). This assumes an individual's subcultural identity is not his or her only one. Often various aspects of oneself are expressed at the same time, yet when putting a look together a person needs to choose which themes will dominate the style of the day. A punk may also be a parent, an office worker, someone who enjoys physical fitness, and/or an avid music enthusiast, and so picking an outfit based on which of these things strikes one as most relevant for that day is important.

Nate articulates the fairly common punk notion of punk as a "true" representation of his identity, whereas dressing for nonpunk contexts, such as work, is a role identity he takes on temporarily. He wants to represent punk in the punk environments, but also beyond and into other contexts if he feels he can get away with it with limited negative ramifications. "I definitely put more effort into what I'm gonna look like outside of work because that's really who I am. And I'd rather show what's on the inside more outwardly even though, not in a flashy way ... I'd rather represent what I'm a part of if I can."

Fig. 3.2 Silk-screened patches expressing identity and identity not (copyright Monica Sklar and Harlo Petoskey).

For punks, it may be that aspects of punk style are incorporated into everyday experiences. Punk can be reflected in an entire outlook and ideology, the way to manage parenting, a workplace, health, and artistic taste. Punk can inform all of these things and thus it may be a salient identity and is always shown, while the other examples may prove less influential on the specific aesthetics of one's daily dress choices. Although these other situations can inform the tone or form of garments, that is, one might wear functionally and socially appropriate attire for a workplace or at the gym, those garments may represent punk aesthetic choices such as color or iconography.

The punk community has always represented diverse upbringings and viewpoints. The combining of varied backgrounds, careers, and interests has historically been a component in the complex makeup of the punk constituency. Yet even though this hodgepodge collection banded together under common ideas and ideals, such as rallying against the same societal issues, each participant remains an individual with his or her own complicated life (Holland 2004; Traber 2008). Therefore the importance of punk style and how it is physically manifested is personally unique and connected to the salience of one's punk identity as compared to other identities.

The significance a person places on an aspect of his identity shapes how that identity is acted out in related behaviors and to what degree it is prioritized.

First, not every social role becomes a part of the self as people assign varied levels of importance to particular roles (Goffman 1959). Second, an individual may assign high value to multiple role identities that may be complementary or competing, potentially leading to emotional skirmishes regarding dress. Consequently, the most salient areas of one's identity become manifest in behaviors such as dress choices for the sake of expression (Stryker 1980; Stryker and Burke 2000). Salient identities may be one's workplace title such as schoolteacher or corporate accountant, and also may be social- or lifestyle-oriented such as a punk with anarchist beliefs or who thrives on skateboarding. Individuals internalize what it means to be a worker or a punk, and those roles become part of their identity. Therefore an individual with a salient punk identity will more likely exert a high level of energy for appropriate role enactment for those roles than for other social roles (Stryker 1980; Stryker and Burke 2000). They may also try to hone in on the particular subgenre of punk dress that best aligns them with the concepts within the subculture they relate to, which is why some punks are crusty while others are emo; each style represent aspects of their identity.

The expression of a punk identity also broadcasts messages about things a punk does not want to associate with. This has been referred to as "identity not" (Freitas et al. 1997), and there is comfort in defining oneself in part by creating a distinction between perceived positives and negatives. This helps establish boundaries of what is punk by proclaiming visually that the punk wearer finds something else offensive or not cool. This can be as bold as wearing a controversially sloganed T-shirt with a blatant message of distaste for a political view or religion, or as subtle as using humor by wearing something a punk would perceive as out of step and repositioning it with irony.

Loss of Individual Identity in Contemporary Society

Wanting to express who you are, and who you are not, has a great deal to do with a motivation to carve out an identity in a complicated culture. In the increasingly fast-paced and multifaceted culture many punks live in, finding and expressing a subcultural identity provides a method to stand out from the noise and to be included in a smaller, more manageable segment within larger society. Notions of individuality are related to that concept, as the pace of the fashion cycle has sped up to a point where underground fashions are being incorporated into the mainstream almost immediately, creating a need to constantly search for tools to express individuality (Woodcock 2006). The development of DIY appearance creates a solution to the loss of identity dilemma because it is unlikely two individuals will come up with the exact same visualization of punk dress.

Many contemporary consumers desire a greater amount of autonomy with their style as compared to past thoughts of strictly following trends and style doctrines, and they want to put a stamp of themselves in their clothing choices

(Campbell 2005). A goal of differentiation from others is a motivating factor for dressing in punk styles. Danielle explained: "What I really like about punk rock fashion is that it is all different. You really don't see five cookie cutter punk rock kids. I mean they might have a lot of the same things but they all wear it in different styles." For Marco, part of the excitement of punk was its fluid and progressive nature: "This thing was exciting because it'd keep changing. I never [said] 'I'm a punk, I'm a punk forever. I'm gonna wear the same thing and listen to the same records forever.' It kept changing" (Interview with author, 2009). This momentum embraces growth and is inclusive of influences and new innovations, which is necessary to separate from a mainstream that is always in a state of flux as well. Also, as the mainstream accepts something that was previously subcultural, that item has a tendency to lose some of its contrarian value, and new positions, including new styles, are needed to express difference.

Being Part of a Subcultural Community

Punk style can exist as a reaction against the mainstream. The wearer can then be positioned as part of a subculture as opposed to being presented as part of the status quo. Dress artifacts represent distaste for the norm, disgust with the mainstream, political and social angst, and artistic expression. Items worn as punk clothing in an effort to show this difference have included garbage bags as dresses, dress for manual labor, vintage clothing, military garb, brothel creeper shoes, blue jeans, fetish wear, and fishnets. Accessories and adornment have included safety pins as closures and jewelry, one-inch logo badges, patches, hair dyed vibrant and unnatural colors and shaped and cut in antimainstream ways, tattoos, piercings, handwritten or screened messages, and the use of wide stripes, black-and-white checkered patterns, and tartan plaids.

Wearing punk style can align one with a past and a culture, a smaller group than the whole of society, as well as the ideals within that group. An individual's participation in a subcultural group or style tribe (Bennett 1999; Polhemus 1996) is a nexus where aesthetic expression functions for individual and social goals. Individuals choose to dress outside the mainstream to express interest in subcultural ideas and provide a tangible link to others who share their lifestyle. Dressing in a personalized version of punk style can also serve to differentiate that person as unique or individual, sometimes even within the punk community. There is a push and pull of dressing "different" and also aligning to preferred aspects of a subcultural community. This utilization of subcultural style is motivated by a desire to draw attention to the notion of kinship among the like-minded in all that is counterculture, provide visual cues regarding ideals and preferences, and/or promote distinction. Roger said: "more than anything it lit a spirit of, not overt anarchy as one would, wanting to overthrow governments, et cetera. But certainly kind of . . . it awakened a voice in people that, 'OK, we don't necessarily have to live by the rules' as it were … Just throwing tradition away left and right, you were really drawn to that" (Interview with author, 2009).

It is possible to express countercultural rebellion through one's attire, however it is also possible to simply present an affectation of an "other" position through clothing and lack sincerity, simply donning what is perceived as an aggressive front without the ideology to support the presentation. It can be a real thought about aesthetics, that even just associating yourself with something it rubs off on you. Marco said: "It's become this sort of icon thing that means you don't have to listen to The Ramones. Which I mean most people are really grateful for. You can just actually wear the T-shirt and it means something, it means you're a rebel. And you've got this kind of rebellious edge" (Interview with author, 2009).

Although subcultural dress is often focused on differentiation from the mainstream as well as alignment with social, musical, and cultural ideas, it is often directed the same way much of fashion is. This comfort in dressing as part of the crowd is a typical part of any fashion cycle and how trends make their way through any group of people, particularly those within a social system.

Peterson commented:

Overall, people are most often influenced by what their friends wear … I remember people sometimes staring at you if you weren't wearing the "right clothing" at the "right show." If anything, the stylistic leaders were probably unintentional. I don't remember any bands writing songs about having to wear certain clothes. That said, hardcore bands' lyrics, and ideas in zines, often influence the way people think. So if a person hears an idea that resonates, and they see the people on stage or in person at a show speaking it, it is natural their eyes would pick up on what they are wearing. (Interview with author, 2011)

Crowds develop similar tastes and follow style leaders within their scene, and individuals succumb to peer pressure about what is accepted. It is a misconception that subcultural style is completely lacking the same framework as mainstream style, as it often is just as prescribed and regimented, and sometimes even more so as it is driven by ideological beliefs, as compared with mainstream's trendy flexibility of going with the flow of fashion cycles. Although even that is a similarity as there are trends too within punk style, which can at times be enforced as almost a social doctrine rather than a fashion magazine suggestion.

Many people, especially youth, like to dress in a similar mode to their friends, demonstrating being part of the crowd through unifying factors that present a stronger whole by group presentation; it also demonstrates the person is on top of trends and in the know about the details of the scene, and for some it can relieve them of what some feel is the burden of uniqueness or individuality. A group of friends dressing alike is very normal, especially in youth culture. Sara said: "Riot

Grrrls in various towns sometimes did dress like each other, thus creating sorts of localized 'Riot Grrrl styles'—not so different from the way many groups of friends tend to dress like alike" (Interview with author, 2011). It is debatable whether the loss of individuality when doing so is a negative or positive, as unique personal communication is sometimes superseded by displays of connectivity and inclusion in a community. Marco said: "It is very easy, like the whole Clash army, the Jam army[2] ... I'm not a punk. I'm just a fan of The Clash. I'm not into fashion; I just dress this way because it is what Clash fans wear. It is a uniform" (Interview with author, 2009). Displays of fandom serve as a form of popular cultural capital built on appreciation and knowledge, showing distinction and discrimination (Fiske 1992).

Postmodern Personalization of Dress

Specific dress artifacts, such as the mohawk or the metal-studded belt, have become iconic even within this amorphous melting pot of style. However the use of bricolage and appropriation has been a core concept of the punk subculture. A hybrid fashion sense could be the result of changing social and political climates, or it could be an agent of change itself. Instead of regimented dress codes, such as in the workplace or for gender roles in society, people now make strategic and personal choices based on religion, situation, and the intended viewer. Therefore people do still show levels of status through high-end accessories, gadgets, and meticulous personal grooming and fitness.

The weight of postmodernism and global influences motivates wearers' punk style. Styled in a certain manner, the bricolage effect meets punk aesthetic norms and draws connections between punk, and its stylistic wearer, with an array of other aspects of culture. This reinforces the idea that it is the individual expressing identity, and a salient punk identity; thus, anything that person wears inherently gets punk essence if they themselves are punk. This is not only shaping why someone might choose the mixed styles that are punk style, as they get to express all sorts of influences simultaneously, but also provides the flexibility not to overly commit to only one part of life, and instead acknowledge life's complexities. However this also explains how so many things can qualify as punk style to its diverse wearers who wear it in a multitude of ways.

It can be hard to tell that a person wearing punk dress may be in a position of power within the workplace because punk style often takes a casual or unconventional aesthetic approach. The goal is often appearing contemporary, and whether this means a hybrid global look or an updated ethnic appearance, Maynard (2004) stressed that people are increasingly self-aware about their visual cues and dress with strategy and purpose.

Fig. 3.3 Postmodern punk style featuring many influences and personalizations, Scotland, 2006 (copyright PYMCA, photographer Mr. Hartnett).

Roger said:

I think that something that's interesting about the English culture is that on the one hand, we get rooted into tradition and not wanting to change things. So on the one hand you don't want to lose that but on the other hand the real kind of movers and shakers are in the fashion world, and what makes this country exciting is they are changing things all the time. And Malcolm and Vivienne were very instigative in that. They came, I think they probably did take a leaf out of some of those '60s design ... like Mary Quant and Biba, who actually turned fashion on its head actually in this country in the '60s because they made it cheap enough for kids to buy, basically, and turned it out in great numbers but changed it every week they would have a new line of stuff in ... The [fashion] seasons, it is like "Fuck the seasons," I mean *every week*. (Interview with author, 2009)

Youth culture is often resistant to categorization and uses clothing in a post-modern manner, sourced numerous ways, not centered in one concept, and often using visual cues that multitask and can be interpreted differently (Henderson and DeLong 2000). The goal is to differentiate against the mainstream and use dress to express a set of ideals and values not limited to the dominant trends and coding systems in Western society.

Furthermore, how each dress item is interpreted has uncertainty in postmodern-ism. The wearer most likely has an intended objective and her version of symbolism attached to the objects; yet the viewer may observe and interpret them differently. Consequently, an item a punk feels maintains his punk self in mainstream contexts may be innocuous to nonpunk viewers if they do not associate punk symbolism with those items; for example, Converse shoes, a plaid miniskirt, or certain tattoos. Similarly, in contexts that are typically hegemonic, such as the workplace, power relationships can be constructed based on who displays the most knowledge of how to act out a role properly. This leads to the notion of communication within punk styles, and how the wearer and the viewer have to negotiate meanings of punk style.

Communicating "Punk" through Dress

Designed objects, such as clothing, are effective tools for communication. Ralph Caplan defines design as "the artful arrangement of materials or circumstances into a planned form" (2005: 23). Design is a reflection of cultural changes as well as an agent of change and they are completely interrelated. Design can also define people through their con-sumption choices and therefore have a cultural impact (Sparke 2004). The twentieth and twenty-first centuries have seen more than one revolution in the way people look at material goods and react and interact with them, including selling and buying.

Punk style is an example of something that is greatly about the design of the item *and* how its wearers and viewers interact with design, all combined with its position within a specific contextual history. Attfield (2000) dubbed this the "object-subject relationship" and stressed its importance in analysis. She argued that, to understand the object-subject relationship, it is important to consider the specifics of the object (such as its aesthetics). In punk, the feel of leather, the rattle of metals, the vibrancy of neons and depths of black, and the familiarity of plaids or exotics of leopard print all do matter. The dynamism of the relationship of people to things is at the core of punk style, in that the symbolism of objects is within the dress and most potent when embodied with sincerity and passion.

This is directly tied to notions about understanding of cues and how to put a look together. The time investment and attention to detail is manifested in two ways. First, there is an investment of daily time to get the right appearance. This is time that is en-joyed. Danielle said: "I really think that punk dress is whatever you're into. If you're into spending three hours or whatever it is on your hair to get some huge mohawk or flat-ironing it straight ... when you have really curly hair, it is spending time." Other

Fig. 3.4 Communicating punk through commitment and attention to dress details, 1984 (copyright Tanya Seeman, photographer Kyle Bradfield).

examples may include getting the hair to the right height, making sure the jewelry creates the perfect accent, or rolling up shirtsleeves to highlight arm tattoos.

Second, while there is credence in the number of minutes or hours spent daily caring about punk, there is greater credence given to those who have spent years or even decades ingrained in the subculture. This highlights true interest and commitment. Many of the dress cues are so subtle only someone who has invested enough time to understand them can identify them. This is a sign of truly being in the community. The details of one's style, including examples such as a small pin referencing a band logo or the color palette that is quite dark with silver accessories, builds the proper aesthetic to express punk identity. The choices may be bold or subdued, and are all about that relationship of wearer, viewer, and the symbolism of the designed object.

Aesthetics, Iconography, and Identity: Communication

To successfully express a punk identity, individuals learn to use the specifics of aesthetics to communicate. The relationship between dress, identity, and environment is strongly tied to how people assign value to each of those components as both wearers and viewers of style. In evaluating aesthetics as it pertains to dress, one can review such concepts as the relationships of the parts to the whole; the organization and order for the viewing process; visual definitions including line, color, and shape (DeLong 1998); and the concepts of appropriation, time, performance, space, and hybridity (Walker Art Center 2007). Identity is largely affected by the aesthetic response an individual has to dress when she takes notice and assigns value to visual, tactile, contextual, and symbolic components (DeLong 1998). Aesthetics affects how individuals interpret dress artifacts as viewers and the way those artifacts are put together by wearers to promote an understanding of the exact symbolism within the design he or she is trying to communicate. When punk dress initially came to fruition, much of it was that gut feeling of what presented the right mood of the times. Marco explained: "we used to go to Let It Rock and buy Chuck Berry sweatshirts. I had no idea who Chuck Berry was, or Gene Vincent … I never heard of any of those people but I just liked the kind of feeling. The aesthetics of it" (Interview with author, 2009).

The specific aesthetic components of dress factor heavily into the identity expression of individuals trying to display a punk ideology. Appearance cues are used by punks as tools for self-expression, to ally with the subculture, to identify with like-minded others, to distinguish themselves from social ideas they dislike, and to be individually creative. Punk dress takes into consideration the aesthetics concept of the part-to-whole relationship regarding the overall form and all of the pieces that compose the form. Nora described how her use of skull-adorned knee socks in her workplace as a teacher greatly differs from how (as she said) "a yuppie chick" would wear knee socks. For a punk it is key to know what details (parts) to select and what complete forms are accepted within punk. This concept is often where cues are employed. The interviewees I spoke with for this research frequently discussed how the look is stylistically composed, which can be subtle or bombastic. The correct use of these cues helps create relationship connections by viewing one another as well as established desired distinctions from one's context.

Expressive and Referential Characteristics

Expressive characteristics are visceral, and arise without thought directly from what is seen (DeLong 1998). For punk it can be the use of sharp lines and lack of fluidity in band logo fonts, leather jacket angles, zippers, tailored 1960s men's suits, or skinny jeans. These sharp lines attempt to make a statement of security, defiance, assuredness, or other evocations of strength and confidence. They are the antithesis of the softness of a flowing floral skirt.

While expressive elements are significant, referential characteristics may be more essential in punk style. Much of punk dress contains referential characteristics based on knowledge about that form's meaning within culture (DeLong 1998). Many punks' dress is a referential mashup of styles adopted from contemporary cultural history, such as the Situationists' handwritten political sloganeering on their clothes and the Rastafarians' dreadlocks, incorporated with touches of individualized preferences and a nod to mainstream trends and functional attire. This results in a great deal of historical referencing through dress to subcultures of the past that influenced or overlap with punk. Many are aware of subcultural history and have adopted various looks from within it, then incorporate things that are distinctly their own, and things that are mainstream, contemporary, and functional. Examples are the beatnik or mod movements, countercultural icons like the Ramones or Bettie Page, and brands preferred by previous subcultures, such as Ben Sherman button-down shirts.

For Tara, the references are targeted to capture a previous point in pop culture and subculture as it relates to her current experience. "I would say now, I still have certain goth leanings that I will dress like sometimes. And the whole kind of Bettie Page '50s thing I like to do, although I like to do my own spin on it and not look exactly like that. But that's the thing I'm most into now is kind of a '50s look." While her references are to time periods and icons of pop culture and subculture history, there are also references to experiences.

Sara explained one example of being referential used by women regarding Riot Grrrls' preference for hair clips in bright colors and featuring bows, rainbows, butterflies, and other ephemera from a girlish youth:

These barrettes were a signifier that went national—Kathleen Hanna[3] often wore bright plastic barrettes at concerts and in photographs, and I think that helped spread the trend. Plastic barrettes were a brilliant signifier because they were so cheap and accessible, also providing a direct link to a childhood which many of the girls, depending on their personal history, longed either to return to (as a time of greater personal confidence) or do over in a more empowered way (for those girls whose childhoods had been marked by abuse). (Interview with author, 2011)

Color is a characteristic within punk style that is both expressive *and* referential. Its expressive characteristics instantly generate reactions in the wearer and for the viewer. Dark colors such as black are used for indicating aggression or secrecy, while neon colors stir excitement. Red is another color frequently used in clothing and hair, which could align with ideas of blood, sex, and heated passion. Referential characteristics in color can draw on known narratives of green indicating social or physical battles of militaries. On the reverse, punks may stay away from pastels or other earth tones that refer to passivity, softness, or compliance, which may counter a punk attitude (Sklar and Michel 2012).

Fig. 3.5 Clad in all black, United States, circa 2000s (copyright Amanda Petoskey).

Symbolic Interaction: Communication

The use of dress to express one's identity is strongly tied to the goal of fostering meaningful interactions. Dress can be used to facilitate connections between people and promote the clear understanding of messages. Roach-Higgins and Eicher (1992) utilized the concept of symbolic interaction when explaining that the symbolism attached to dress provides a communication tool to strongly express identity. Then, through the tool of dress, wearers and observers are aided in their interactions based on their perceptions and evaluations.

Punk style by its very nature has always had great variation regarding dress objects and design symbolism. Hebdige stated that in subcultures such as punk, the ideology of the lifestyle was aligned with the aesthetic design elements of the clothes and graphics as well as the vocal and rhythmic aggressive sonics of the music. However, he noted that while the theme remained consistent, the method would vary as no component was fixed and no item deemed sacred. Through this blend of stability and change, Hebdige points out, semioticians have had trouble dealing with "the absence of permanent signifiers" (1979: 115). In addition to the fluidity of the imagery and iconography within punk dress, the subculture has also become commercialized and widely distributed, now available at chain stores located in most shopping malls.

The core symbolism of punk style has the potential to change through each era's adaptations on product diffusion and cultural acceptance. Therefore benign objects can be turned punk through proper use of aesthetic cues, and many formerly punk-centric cues such as metal studs can be worn in nonpunk ways.

However it is worth reiterating that, because much of punk dress historically started as nonpunk items repurposed through bricolage, it is complicated to say when those items turn back into not being punk that they are appropriation. It only becomes that when worn in a way that resembles the punk aesthetic and that seems to share some of the surface level motivations of shock or alignment with subculture or at least music cultures, yet it does not maintain its embodiment; versus much of punk's bricolage or appropriation was completely redoing items' usage for new purposes. Deciphering the aesthetic value and symbolism engraved within the object is complicated with design, such as with punk dress, which is continually reinvented and simultaneously copied, as well as adjusted for fluid social meanings.

Social Meanings

Dress can express a punk's opinion of society and how one wants to demonstrate his or her place in the world. The aesthetics, cues, and symbolism can construct identity and

Fig. 3.6   Padlock necklace worn by female (copyright Monica Sklar).

express it, can promote ideas, and can place a person within society through nonverbal communication. Ideas projected include class, race, gender, politics, and social status. There are social meanings in dress, as related to the aesthetic cues—the symbolism—and that is how people gather the wearer's statements on things like politics, relationships, and kinship to others such as participation in a particular subculture.

The Viewer

The development of punk style takes into consideration the viewer and the context. The viewer "is the observer of the form." This could be a third party or the wearer himself when he evaluates his own image (DeLong 1998: 16). Punks participate in viewing of themselves and others, and manipulate their appearance according to the situation. They are often quite reflexive about dressing as a result of self-viewing, and have a strong awareness of how they may be viewed by others. The goal is to effectively communicate ideas through their style choices. There is also often a desire to be viewed as one's true self, which many associate with their punk identity, but this is of greater concern when self-viewing than when being viewed by others. The salient punk identity frequently means there is prioritization in self-viewing over third-party viewing, as remaining comfortable in one's own shoes is vital.

Viewer as Self

There are multiple sides to viewing. The first is the viewer as himself. The punks interviewed commented that they view themselves often and try to think of reactions that might be generated. They also consider levels of their own emotional comfort as related to being pleased with how one views himself or herself. An example of being concerned with reactions from others based on how you view yourself came from Stacey: "That's kind of weird that I myself am self-conscious and worried about how I'm portrayed to other people but I really don't care too much about what other people would think. It is more what I think." Ben elaborated, saying, "I'd rather like the way I look or be happy with it than somebody else be happy with it."

There are striking issues with emotional discomfort rooted in the idea of not being "yourself," particularly with regard to efforts to function in nonpunk contexts and to dress appropriately in those contexts. Katie explained her quest for emotional comfort as related to dress: "I've always been searching for a style that I feel most comfortable in, that I kind of feel is a reflection of just kind of how you feel on the inside." Denise added: "I like to feel comfortable in what I'm wearing because it just, I think it just speaks to kind of who I am."

Punks are individuals who originally did not fit within the confines of society, and through persistent searching found that the subculture was an outlet to express their identity. Although punk style allows room for individual expression and linking to a culture that differs from the mainstream, there is still a sense of judgment that must be grappled with. Augie explained: "I don't mind being on parade on my own terms. I don't like being on parade when someone pulls me aside and all of a sudden I'm on show ... So that's kind of negative." Consequently, many do not feel wholly comfortable in the mainstream, and make a great effort to find a place in society that makes sense for who they are. Marla summarized finding the balance between expressing oneself and not going so far that one isn't comfortable either. She said: "I want to be comfortable. And part of being comfortable is not looking like I'm coming way out of left field. But then I don't want to look like a soccer mom either. So it can be a fine line."

Punks Viewed by Others

The wearer is also concerned with being viewed by others. Punks respond to how they feel they are being viewed and to internalized perceptions of the implications generated from one's appearance and how others perceive it. When donning punk dress, the wearer picks up on the reactions of others and interprets positive and negative reactions from them, and they have mixed opinions about these reactions. A range of emotions can result for the punk based on perceived viewer reaction and what the wearer was trying to get across with his or her dress.

There can be apathy when the punk claims not to care what the reaction is to his or her appearance, as expressed by Stacey: "seriously, it is like I just don't care anymore about dressing up for anyone." There can also be happiness that a look was positively received if that was the intended goal. This is particularly true if it is not solely a compliment that boosts one's ego about one's physical appearance, which punks are often not above appreciating, but the happiness is magnified when it represents a connection sparked with another person. Jonathan exemplified this when he said: "If I'm at a show and I'm wearing some band shirt, some guy's like 'Hey, that's a great band.' It is nobody that nobody's ever heard of. 'Sweet, man,' kind of made that instant connection."

Negative reactions can be more complicated. Unintended negative reactions can lead to disappointment for the wearer. However, there can also be a sense of joy for the punk when a negative reaction *was* the intended outcome. In certain circumstances one can relish the feeling of making others uncomfortable. Augie relived a particular example:

> I was riding ... on my motorbike with a few friends and I had this sleeveless [his band] shirt, and just seeing all of those like ultra-rich mansions around there, I was concerned with how they perceived me because I hope they perceived me as a threat whether I was or not. I mean I'm not. But I like the idea of being like the rebel on the motorbike who, like the long hair, tattoos, sleeveless shirt and whatever skulls and shit like that. Because I thought maybe some people would get the wrong idea or whatever. And it is kind of fun to be in like a motorbike gang, driving around or riding around. So in that instance, it was a conscious decision ... I was like, I'll go fuck with some rich people.

Fig. 3.7 Communication and connections made through different forms of punk style (copyright Amanda Petoskey).

Perhaps it is retribution for years of being made to feel uncomfortable by people in the mainstream. Nora describes her initial feelings of this nature:

> Being the kid walking down the hall in all black with combat boots on and red eyeliner and half my head shaved. The looks I got and the reaction I got from people ... they got the fuck out of my way ... [this] was I would say my first almost tangible positive experience because that was good. That was exactly what I needed for that time and place.

On the contrary, a positive reaction can elicit goodwill toward the punk even though it was not the wearer's original intention. He could be trying to send one message with his attire, but it can be interpreted incorrectly and have a reaction that benefits him anyway. Punks know their aesthetics will not always be interpreted as intended, and so sometimes they are flexible on how hard they strive to communicate effectively, and occasionally are even appreciative of whatever attention is received.

Punks Viewing Others

In addition to viewing the self and being viewed by others, punks view others in society, such as those considered mainstream. When punks view others they can have strong reactions, both positive and negative, often resulting in evaluations of others based on dress. The punks expressed that they often find others dress poorly, look uncool, sloppy, dirty, unfashionable, overly sexualized, and generally inappropriate per context. It is not a one-way relationship of victimhood of the disenfranchised that then strives to offend the person giving the initial judgment. It is also about an assessment of the mainstream coming from the punk's standpoint. True, judging each other by the way we look is human nature, however there is a stereotype that the punk is solely reactionary because of being judged, and also a peacock on display to be gazed at, and it is more mutual. It is not that they gather to mock the mainstream, but they have a critical eye for a well-styled person, a sloppily adorned person, a person in or out of trends, or who perhaps does things outside the punk ideology as well (for a vegan punk, seeing a person wearing fur might be a point of judgment, although it is not always such an obvious example). Although punks' interpretation of fashion may differ from the mainstream, they express a clear understanding of contextual appropriateness, and they feel others often fall outside those boundaries, whether it is regarding workplace appropriateness or everyday casual attire. The notion of the viewer is a complicated one as there is a desire to be viewed by the proper use of symbols, which have societal meanings, and yet one does not want to be pigeonholed, especially in a negative way, regarding those meanings.

Punk Style and Context

Context plays a large role in punk style choices by the wearer and the subsequent viewer interpretations. Context is both physical, such as: "immediate physical space or environment and how all aspects of this space interact with the clothed body" (DeLong 1998: 18), and cultural, including "date, time, and place, as well as the values and ideals of a society" (DeLong 1998: 18). There are certain arenas where there are social expectations. These expectations are often about roles (Goffman 1959) and sometimes about things like status or function like a job task. Punk dress aspires to fit within these contexts as best it can. Often punks are trying to "be themselves" yet still fit into what is expected from them in mainstream contexts. Punks are aware of the overall idea of cultural and physical contexts, and generally attempt to dress accordingly. For some dressing contextually means almost creating a visual persona attuned to each environment so that he or she is perfectly aligned to the situation. Punk style is not as rigid as may be hypothesized, and punks often attempt to match their dress behaviors to be appropriate per context.

Physical Context

The physical contexts described by interviewees can be divided into four categories: Punk, Work, Everyday, and Other. They are tangible spaces in which punks spend their time and have experiences, and each is filled with sociocultural components.

Punk Context

The punk context includes going to bars, music shows, festivals and events, record stores, sports such as skateboarding, and general hanging out with friends. Denise is a punk who dresses somewhat differently depending on where she is headed. She said, "If I'm going to a concert or something, I might wear something different than if I'm going to watch people skateboarding or something like that."

Physical comfort is a functional factor when dressing for the punk context in addition to the emotional comfort of successful identity expression. The punk context can include physically unrestrictive garments such as T-shirts, jeans, and athletic shoes. This is as compared to the notion of formal attire for somewhere such as a workplace or special occasion, clothing such as suits and high heels, often perceived as uncomfortable because of being tight and restrictive. However, Stacey discussed how physical comfort could also be sacrificed in the punk context to increase emotional comfort, identity expression, and even physical safety, because of the shell-like protective qualities of some punk garments. Examples of punk context attire that may be physically uncomfortable are heavy leather jackets and pants (although once broken in they can be quite body conforming, warm, and comfortable), bondage wear, dense layers, heavy steel-toed boots, and immobile strongly sprayed/glued hairstyles. These garments can be more physically uncomfortable than casual garments such as T-shirts and jeans, but the increase in emotional comfort is due to their blocking out the mainstream world.

A sense of practicality does factor into the choices for the punk context. Chrissy discussed the hassle of certain garments and the potential for physical harm due to a crowded situation:

> Normally the shows where I wanted to be up at the front, I always made sure I had good shoes … I'm not wearing anything that I care about getting beer spilled on or ripped or stolen. And you know, that actually, the show thing changed too when [her city] became non-smoking. Because there were definitely certain items I would not wear to a club because the smell would last and linger and if it was a vintage item or something that couldn't be cleaned easily, I didn't want to risk ruining it.

Work Context

In the work context, the interviewees described their dress using phrases such as appropriate, inappropriate, neat, well groomed, clean, lacking distress or signs of wear, feminine, utilitarian, business casual, and business formal. Factors such as wanting flattering and fashionable attire that looks appropriate for their role, as well as the tasks at hand for that day, and any other factors such as season all combined to make their workplace appearance.

Nate said:

> I don't really push the limits of the dress code or what's accepted. I would feel kind of affronted if I had to really conform in this really buttoned up kind of manner. But I do try to make it obvious when I can that "Hey, I'm into punk rock" … But when I'm at work, yeah. I try to conform with the expectations.

A workplace associated with mainstream society can function as a reliving of the experimentation experienced in one's youth, as many punks have to find a way of comfortably presenting themselves all over again. However in adulthood they have some of the confidence that comes with age; they know that punk brings them closer to a comfortable sense of self.

Everyday Context

The everyday context refers to private time at one's own house, going to run errands, and casual and personal social activities involving family and friends. Sean and Matt note that this third context has dress that slightly differs from work and punk, but is more closely aligned with punk.

> Kicking around the house, I'll wear a Hawaiian shirt. And generally they're a little bit more edgy or whatever, but … that kind of identity is a little more laid back.—Sean

> On a typical day when I come home from work, I want to just change into jeans and a T-shirt or something like that, just to be comfortable and not worry about getting things on myself.—Matt

The everyday context is neither the blatant self-expression nor subcultural affiliation of punk environments, nor is it the rigid appropriateness and possible conformity of work. It involves a loosened concern for viewer perception and includes choices such as jeans, sweats, T-shirts, no makeup, and not shaving. Some punks explained the everyday context was closely tied to the punk contexts, as punk was so all encompassing in their identity they wear punk dress everywhere.

Zhac described how her everyday style has evolved:

> There used to be a time in my life when I was doing really elaborate stuff with my makeup and my appearance. I used to wear these crazy headscarves and I would paint my whole face. And I couldn't leave my house without doing all that, even if it was just to go down to the corner store, you know. And that could take up to an hour to do all of that just to walk a couple blocks. So I'm probably not that concerned anymore. You know, I can go to the store without any makeup, with my hair sticking up kind of funny and just throw some sunglasses on and fuck anybody who looks at me funny.

As punks mature, they wear punk dress more specifically in punk contexts, and the everyday is often a casual and laid-back version of punk dress, or not correlated to punk dress much at all. It is toned down, but not for the same reasons punks tone down punk dress for the workplace.

Other Contexts

The remaining situations fall into another category and include events that require some version of formal attire such as weddings, family occasions, and romantic dates. These contexts may include garments from punk dress, work dress, everyday dress, or altogether different items. Chrissy, Augie, and Nate explain how they dress for such contexts:

> Because my comfort and my identity sometimes does need to be shown a little differently in different settings … Going to see my husband's grandmother, who we haven't seen for a little while … I'm wearing shorts and a T-shirt and he kind of puts on like a nice button-down to go see her. Looks at me and says, "Are you going to wear that?" And I'm wearing a Dischord[4] T-shirt. And I'm like "Oh, if I was going to my family's house I wouldn't have thought about it," but going to his family's house and I'm like "OK, I'll put something else on" … So I have my conscience and my thoughts about how I dress. Then there's what's appropriate, that sometimes I need reminders.—Chrissy

> If I was going out with a girl I'd be more concerned about how she could potentially perceive me. It is kind of a case-by-case basis. I am aware of people's reactions but it doesn't mean that if someone didn't like something, it would probably egg me on to do it more than it would be to make me change it.—Augie

> If I was going to a wedding obviously I dressed up. I tucked in my wallet chain in the pockets so that wasn't poking out, and didn't look rough or whatever. So that's about it. I suppose if I was going out on a date, I wouldn't wear a Poison Idea T-shirt, which I like that band, I wouldn't wear the shirt because it is not really appropriate. I'd probably wear something a little bit nicer because, just out of respect for the person I was going out with and to show them that I actually care about the situation and not like, "Oh here's something I picked up off the floor." So that's pretty much it, otherwise I pretty much wear the same basic thing everywhere I go except for some of those exceptional situations.—Nate

Situations such as formal occasions are strongly tied to a viewer and ideas about perceptions. Interviewees described adhering to social expectations as a priority over expressing a normally salient punk identity. Suits and cocktail dresses may be the norm for an evening wedding, yet the way those appearances are stylized may reflect punk aesthetics, particularly in the small details. There is some room in the development of an outfit for identity expression, and this is important, for instance, on a romantic date with a desire to build connections through visually demonstrating one's psyche and tastes. However, yielding to the prevailing styles of that context does sometimes supersede punk aesthetics and in these often formal additional contexts that are easily categorized as work, punk, or everyday, a punk may choose to go with prescribed attire rather than try to forge a middle ground of punk style and contextual appropriateness. However, the display of piercings, tattoos, and unconventional hair dye can provide that balance of the salient punk identity shining through even when the punk was attempting to comply with conventions.

Blurring Contexts

There is a conflicted mix of pride and apprehension regarding punk dress overlapping into nonpunk contexts. There is some fear of negative ramifications of punk dress having poor reception from viewers in nonpunk contexts. The same viewer may show up in multiple contexts and therefore the punk style wearer may exhibit caution in their choices. Nora explained that she reduces how revealing her miniskirt, fishnet stockings, or thigh-high socks may be—her preferred attire when she is going somewhere that is a punk context, such as a music show—when she worries she may run into someone from her work context.

In this age of online social networking, the lines between the boundaries of contexts are becoming increasingly blurred. It is common to hear of employers checking photos on Facebook and other sources on the Internet for "bad behavior." For some punks this is a cause for concern. Ben faced an extreme example of the ramifications of this when his job came into question because of public nudity that was an expression of his punk style in a punk context, yet seen by members of his work context through social media. He explained:

> We were playing this show in Boston and I decided to take off my clothes and just try to make people feel uncomfortable at the gig or whatever. But there were some photo-journalists there that took pictures. They wound up in the zines; they wound up on the Internet. But all you could see was me from the waist up. You couldn't see anything that would have been … private … But people where I was working at the time … I was working like a 9 to 5 job behind a desk, saw it … they did some research on me. I try to keep my band life and my work life separate. But they found it and they printed them out and circulated them. And I ended up losing my job because of it.

Cultural Context

Cultural contexts can include demographics such as race, marital status, ethnicity, and geography, and they can include social constructs related to gender or economics. How an individual internalizes gender and age roles, ethnic influences, and class backgrounds, for example, will sway aspects of how they choose to dress. Generally those parameters are socially constructed and not formally inscribed to the point of dress codes. However one's interpretation can feel as though there is rigidity. The punk ideology is inclined to debate the boundaries shaping cultural contexts, and yet the debate itself in some ways continues to reinforce their social relevance, and this can spur a reaction resulting in punk dress. Apathy is more rare, and the most common is probably to balance some aspects of punk ideas and aesthetics with some dress behaviors prescribed within a cultural context.

Age

The process of aging changes one's attitudes toward dress. Punk is a subculture that one does not have to grow out of, as it is ideological as much as it is situational (going to shows, buying records, etc.). Therefore punks do still express a punk spirit in their physical representation but it may be adjusted with time. However the punk look, whether it is the loud iconic style or the ultra-casual hardcore presentations, has associations with youth in mainstream culture. This interpretation is on the part of the viewer who may associate those styles with disdain for convention, authority, structure, or refinement. The youthful association is also generated from the wearer as interviewees explained that when they were younger they felt a need to be more shocking through dress, as a form of self-expression. However, the interviewees described a shift that came with age.
    Nate explained:

> The kind of stuff I was doing ten years ago when I was young, I didn't know any better and I was more into like "Hey, look at me. I want attention and look how different I am from you," and maybe being different just to be different or being extreme just to be extreme. And that's not something I can really relate to nowadays. Maybe that's part of getting older and maturing.

As punks get older, they are more flexible to blending into nonpunk contexts such as in their everyday experiences. They run a cost-benefit analysis, and many decide there is value in not being confrontational in nonpunk contexts, such as a workplace, and consider punk dress confrontational as it is considered outside the norm (Sklar and DeLong 2012). However, when they discuss the benefits of blending in at work they often couple it with the statement that blending in does not necessarily mean they are giving up their punk values.

The Mainstream

The concept of punk exists as a cultural context with social parameters and as a physical context with locations for participation. Thus the mainstream can be positioned in a similar manner as an opposing or different context than punk. *Mainstream* is a fluid term and varies internationally and throughout history, but can be assessed as the dominant social culture and its resulting mores.

Mainstream culture has reigning style trends that the masses partake in, and a punk may choose to utilize some of these as well as disregard others with varying levels of enthusiasm in either direction. There may be adoption of some mainstream stances, and distaste for others that go against a punk ideology, including punk visual norms. The mainstream as a culture is then represented publically (physically) in spaces such as shopping malls, workplaces, and family-friendly functions within which the punk decides whether to blend in or stand out and what the cultural implications will be of his or her decision.

Gender

Gender issues, and correlated issues of sexuality, factor into cultural contexts. When choosing how to present punk styles, particularly within nonpunk contexts, often there is consideration of gender norms and expectations (Sklar and DeLong 2012). Rachel explained the challenges of appearing too sexualized somewhere such as her workplace as a teacher. In those contexts she downplays her sexuality through shoe and clothing choices. Nonetheless, she still was reprimanded when she took off her sweater and her shirt was cut in such a way her cleavage was revealed upon bending down.

Gender roles and stereotypes in dress can be considered from many angles. In a hypothetical discussion about what type of shoes she should wear to teach, and trying to imagine the criticism she would get if she wore Dr. Martens, Marla said she considers what would be comfortable and good for her feet. She imagines in her academic workplace the principal might say: "Well, you're a woman, you shouldn't dress that way." Marla spoke of androgyny and professionalism intertwined. She does not want to look too sexualized yet feels appearing too masculine also makes others uncomfortable. Her goals for comfort and style raise questions about perceptions of gender stereotypes.

Jonathan expands on this when he explains the disdain he receives when wearing casual skateboard athletic shoes in his law office workplace, as compared to his female coworkers who do not receive reprimands:

> If I'm not in court, I wear my tennis shoes all the time. And people really were like "What are you doing? Why are you wearing tennis shoes or whatever." Even though all the girls are allowed to do it, the guys can't do it. So I still do it. It is kind of a nice "f*%! you" ... They'll wear tennis shoes. Like when they get out, they take their heels off or whatever. I've seen some of them wear tennis shoes in court. And they seem to get away with it and, or they don't wear any shoes around the office.

Jonathan feels his female coworkers are allowed some freedom from wearing formal shoes because heels are known to be uncomfortable, even though the same may be said of men's formal shoes. Both Marla and Jonathan expressed desires to enact a vision of professionalism with punk flair and are boxed in somewhat by gender expectations of what is acceptable for them to wear. Jonathan perceives that women's shoes represent a relief from the discomforts of heels while as a male his are more tied to concepts of laziness, dirtiness, or being contrarian.

Punks regularly try to dress contextually, both physically and culturally. They actively manipulate their appearance to suit the environment and their role within a given situation. They want to express their identity in a way that achieves personal goals within a context, as nearly anyone would. This may result in dressing "age appropriately" in a cultural context, dressing like "management" in a work context, or dressing "cool" in a punk context (Sklar and DeLong 2012).

Personal Feelings of Confidence in Context

The way one dresses in physical and cultural contexts is inspired by how secure and confident one is in the situation (Sklar and DeLong 2012). This is true for dressing professionally and socially, and influences emotional and physical comfort. Gaining a desired position professionally or socially is connected with the idea of "viewer" and also heavily reflects on context. For contexts such as the workplace, dressing appropriately can contribute to career success, as seen in positive outcomes including respect from coworkers and promotions. The interviews indicated some punks feel there are benefits to dressing to reflect their role in their workplace. This potentially leads to other aspects of happiness in life that can overlap with punk perhaps from financial comfort or high self-esteem. Therefore Rachel and others take into consideration how punk dress is incorporated (or not) into workplace dress. Rachel said: "I think I definitely have tried to adapt my wardrobe so that it is appropriate. Because I also want to be viewed as a professional."

The implications are similar within the punk subculture. There are concerns about having the right standing and properly representing that position. Formal workplace attire, such as blouses, business suits, and ties are rarely transferred to a punk context because of their physical discomfort and also because of potentially appearing "uncool" or "dorky." Exceptions are sometimes made for subgenres of punk that have trends in formal dress and crossover subcultures such as mods. Overall, though, formal attire in the conventional Western sense rarely overlaps. Casual workplace attire, particularly that for physical labor, is accepted, and is sometimes worn in punk contexts by those who do not partake in jobs of that nature. This debate over what workplace dress is appropriate in punk speaks to some of the challenges of class and elitism that are complicated within the punk ideology.

Punks are aware that the same garment that provides benefits and increases one's standing in one context potentially decreases it in another setting. Additionally, regarding one's confidence within a context, the more a punk invests in time commitment to that subculture the less he feels the need to use aesthetics for identity expression of his participation in the community. Nate describes this issue:

> It is definitely more casual the way I dress now, compared to how I was when I was younger. Maybe [I was] a little less secure about being a punk rocker now that I've felt like I paid my dues more and I know, I'm secure in my position in the scene and everything. And I know what I do is important and valuable to the punk rock community, I don't feel like I need to be as visually obvious or I guess stereotype or cliché.

In some situations, punks have gained a desired position or spent enough time invested in the environment that they can express themselves more flexibly. Some explain that they start dressing in one manner, and, as they grow more confident in their position in the noncontext, feel they can incorporate more of their punk self and see less need to conform to what they originally perceived as appropriate for work. This was demonstrated by Nora who said she no longer wears floral skirts, and Tara, who dressed conventionally when she moved to a new city for the sake of a positive first impression.

At a white-collar workplace it is not uncommon to perpetually need to represent oneself in a visually appropriate manner, and often workplace dress becomes more rigid as one goes further up the professional ladder. While this is the opposite of the tactic in punk contexts, Audra indicated she is comfortable with this process as her identity is increasingly defined by her work and/or overall self-confidence in any environment regardless of dress. Audra said: "I'm comfortable enough with myself and my lifestyle that it doesn't bother me to express myself in a conservative wardrobe similarly to how I express myself in a punk type wardrobe."

Negotiations Regarding Appearances

A punk is generally very in tune with the relationship of his identity to his visual style, as well as to viewer perceptions, including self-perceptions. That strong self-awareness of presenting symbolic cues within contextual expectations is a delicate balance, and sometimes figuring it all out leads to tension. The phrase "appearance labor" names the push and pull felt when making tough dress choices. "Appearance labor" is a "certain amount of physical and mental effort on the part of the attire wearer, a certain amount of dissonance between what individuals believe that they are expected to wear and what they would prefer to wear" (Peluchette, Karl, and Rust 2006: 50). Punks go through this to some extent, particularly with aging bodies, with workplace expectations, and with changing lifestyles. Therefore, punks frequently engage in some type of negotiation regarding their punk style to achieve their most desirable outcome (Sklar and DeLong 2012). The amount of strain varies depending on the exact individuals and situation. Appearance labor does exist, however it is not as strenuous as may be hypothesized. Punks greatly reduce any strain by exercising savvy internal negotiations and come up with strategies that guide their dress behaviors (Sklar and DeLong 2012).

One accommodation punks use to overcome appearance labor includes deciding when to blend in and when to stand out visually. They adjust their appearance to blend in or stand out based on viewer perceptions and context. Often punks are selective about what they reveal and what they conceal regarding their punk identity and its related visual cues. This results in stylistic modifications such as reducing cosmetics and accessories, wearing band and statement logos that are graphic but not with text, as well as covering tattoos. Punks use dress to attract or repel viewers, or even to slip into the background. Stacey discussed trying to blend in at her office: "Pretty much I always wear my hair down. Like I said, not a lot of makeup. Not really anything outstanding. That's all I can pretty much say. Pretty much I try to blend into the background as much as possible. Slide under the radar" (Sklar and DeLong 2012).

At the workplace one may try to be discreet, yet in a punk context the goal may be to stand out or at least to feel each item represents one's taste. Tara discussed her efforts when she said:

> Dressing more to like stand out and taking more attention to what I wear, not just throwing on jeans and a sweater, but actually you know, layering things on, lots of accessories. I guess I just take more time when I'm doing that than I do in my everyday wear.

Within the idea of blending in and standing out one option is to pick and choose when to push social boundaries with clothing choices. Audra discussed her method for wearing her punk style yet having it less recognizable to those who are not in the know: "I wear plugs [stretched earrings that look like large studs] to work. But they have to be plugs that don't appear to be plugs. Yes I wear my tongue ring, but that's because you don't see it when I'm speaking at a meeting or something like that." Audra's piercings are part of the body modification that accompanies much of contemporary subculture yet for someone who is unfamiliar they simply look like average earrings.

Sometimes there is a joy is stretching the limits of punk identity expression within a circumstance where that may not be the norm. Emotional and physical comfort are accomplished by developing an awareness of the boundaries within a context, and then figuring out how to function within or outside of them, all while achieving whatever the desired goals were in that situation. Zhac summarized her strategy: "I don't really resist it so much as I just try to blur the edges of it, you know and so far I've been pretty successful with it and in my previous jobs as well as in my current job. My clothes are always clean, they're not wrinkled, they fit well. But I try not to be boring." Negotiating what to wear may not be as simple as either complying or rebelling, as sometimes the norms within a context can be vague, and/or the expectations may be fairly obvious; however a punk's outlook or standards may differ from the mainstream point of view regarding how a dress choice should be handled (Sklar and DeLong 2012).

A contrasting method to blending in or standing out is the option to tone punk style down to be less obvious. Once boundaries in a certain situation are established, one punk may push the shock limits while another punk may retreat by toning down the visual volume. Either of these choices will result in a decision of how much of a punk identity to visually reveal or conceal, through tattoo and piercing exposure, texture and pattern/iconography options, and garment fit/proportions. Sometimes the aging process motivates toning down one's punk style. This may result in not wanting to wear short skirts as one did when younger. New versions of punk style are then developed through this maturation that suit changing bodies and contexts. Other shifts in dress choices may be driven by the need to dress on a budget and attempts to buy clothing that can function in an array of contexts as both punk and nonpunk (Sklar and DeLong 2012).

Punks also navigate between blending in and standing out by using creativity to develop and maintain their entire wardrobe. Some purchase two separately themed wardrobes, literally dividing their clothes into punk and nonpunk. Marla said, "I might wear a flowered shirt to work, but probably not out socially." They use the appropriate clothing per context although the choices generally reflect their overall taste rather than completely donning a front of new selves to slip into depending on which closet they mine. Work attire may have mainstream appeal while their everyday and punk contexts showcase their more patent punk looks (Sklar and DeLong 2012).

Others prefer to establish one wardrobe filled with garments that can merge punk and nonpunk clothing concepts into a blended look. The core items in this consolidated closet are versatile garments that can multitask in varied contexts. Often small changes in hosiery, shoes, or accessories can swing the same core clothing pieces toward punk or nonpunk presentations. Examples may be plaid skirts or Dr. Martens shoes (not boots) that have a benign appearance, but when styled with key aesthetic pieces like fishnet tights or black skinny jeans, they can easily lean toward expressing a punk identity. Wearing a punk garment in the same ensemble as a mainstream garment is another method to having one wardrobe. These individuals creatively piece together an integrated look each day mixing business suits with rainbow hair and demure sweater twin sets in leopard print (Sklar and DeLong 2012).

All of this takes into consideration buying on a budget, which is aligned with the responsibilities of aging. Punks have to consider how many clothing items they can afford and a garment's versatility. Tara said:

> I would say like, most of the clothes I wear or buy, I can wear to work. I mean there are certain things I buy that are go out dancing things, but that's a very small part of my wardrobe ... I mean even with casual Fridays, you can wear jeans to work. So there isn't a whole lot, maybe some T-shirts and stuff that I can't wear to work.

This differs from the way younger punks dress who tend to use disposable income to visually express themselves very blatantly, without regard to the cost of the clothes or whether they were multipurpose (Sklar and DeLong 2012).

Conclusions

While there is not a definitive answer to the question of why some individuals wear punk style, themes related to culture and context drive the choices. The lasting physical styles include general aesthetic parameters that tend to be followed such as chunky, black, and silver, and that also include specific garments such as boots, fishnets, and T-shirts. Although the tangible form and the aesthetics of the garments worn as a person's punk style are important, overall themes describing punk dress were often culturally or motivationally oriented related to attitude, kinship, time commitment, and differentiation from others.

Punks focus on motivating factors such as creative expression, communication, perceptions, and attitude, all per context, more so than maintaining a prescribed uniform in all situations. Thus there is flexibility and subtlety that is contrary to the stereotype. Self-identification with the punk subculture influences how they go about making the specific dress choices to reflect their identity within a context, but being punk does not exist completely outside acknowledgment of the context around them. They are fully aware of the varied contexts of their life, and dress in a conscious and thoughtful way to make the most out of each situation. Punks frequently express their subcultural leanings as a dominant aspect of their entire identity; yet they do not dress in one punk fashion in every environment. They are flexible and attentive to contextual needs, running frequent cost-benefit analyses to determine how punk dress relates to a context.

Punk style is often about the viewer as self (personal expression) in conjunction with the viewer as a third party, and only mildly to do with dressing for social expectations. Punks do dress to meet punk norms, but also feel dress freedom within those parameters. The punk context takes into consideration the desire to express oneself with emotional and physical comfort blended together. Dressing for work involves more concern for social role expectations and third-party viewer opinions. There is a willingness to forego some emotional and physical comfort to achieve workplace benefits. A higher level of sacrifice is acceptable within the workplace than it is within the punk context. Through the creative use of accommodations, and because of postmodern influence on punk dress, many punks successfully alleviate appearance-related labor issues.

Punk dress is built on cultural hallmarks going hand in hand with some specifics of form. However, loss of cultural identity is a greater concern than loss of a particular visual signifier. Hence, those able to manipulate dress creatively with form to express punk cultural hallmarks and cues experience decreased appearance labor. Therefore punks find ways to make their style perform for them. Just as some have found a way to reference punk iconography within a work-appropriate wardrobe, many punks find this double coding within acceptable norms a successful merging of visual representations of punk and nonpunk contexts.

–4–

Punk Style and Society

While shopping in London's Camden Market, the famed subcultural shopping district, I found every kind of punk ware for sale. Clash T-shirts and studded bracelets were displayed from stall to store to vendor up and down the district. At first it was a blast, an overload to my counterculture senses, but by afternoon it slipped into a disconcerting blur, reeking of overcommodification, and by the time I left I had only bought a necklace that looks like a cassette tape, two pairs of patterned athletic shoelaces, and lunch. I was awestruck by the huge selection of anything punk I could want set right before me, and yet, in that quantity and with so much duplication it seemed somehow un-punk. Lost was the DIY factor of something hand embellished, or the personalization a garment gains when worn in for years. Removed was the satisfaction of self-curating the perfect item from a vintage shop or even a mainstream store that somehow exudes just the right amount of punk expression on me personally. Although Camden Market was lacking in certain sentiments, it was in fact heartwarming to see so many things I consider my taste and relevant to subculture compiled in one place. I left conflicted. I had always thought Camden would be a treasure chest of shopping delight, but my initial reaction was a mix of thrill and a funny taste in my mouth.

What was the embedded meaning of a reproduction concert T-shirt sold at two for $10? What about the tourists gawking and taking pictures in front of the oversized Dr. Martens shoe on an awning (admittedly including myself)? Sure I knew that awning was for a storefront that was one of the first to sell Dr. Martens to punks and that helped establish the brand as a fundamental part of punk style, but the umpteenth rack of plaid bondage pants overshadowed even those special benchmarks of punk style's history.

I was mildly cynical, although not completely disgruntled as the beautiful weather and general fun of the trip could not truly dampen my enjoyment. When I returned home to the States I regretted not buying more while there. While it is not entirely difficult to get punk-styled items in the mid-sized American city where I live, it is hard to find the exact items I may want, right at my fingertips, and reasonably priced. I also recalled Camden Market's artists' booths, the unique vintage items, and the sheer volume as having potential to build a lot of fun wardrobe items, not just the one-stop-punk-identity-shop I saw it as at the time. Perhaps during my brief trip it was just one of those situations where too many choices is worse than too few and I became overwhelmed (Schwartz 2003).

As time passed I began to feel in retrospect that something about buying a repro-duction Clash T-shirt at Camden Market was inherently cooler than buying the same shirt at a chain store in my local shopping mall. This is true even if, for all I know, similar manufacturers produce the garment. Somewhere on the spectrum of ways to acquire punk goods, the shopping experience both disappointed and excited me, and when placed in context against the appropriated punk images I saw throughout my domestic shopping trips to major malls in the United States, Camden Market did seem mostly geared toward exploiting its own audience rather than getting a new wearer through misappropriated or newly redesigned images.

My shopping excursions raised the issue of whether it is better to take main-stream items and reconfigure them in aesthetic combinations that then appear punk or whether it is better to consume prescribed punk attire. And if the latter, whether that premade punk attire should come from punk or nonpunk sources. A band T-shirt or distressed skirt that is homemade, sold at Camden Market, at the Mall of America, or at an independent boutique may all look similar, however part of punk style is the way in which the garment was produced, the symbolism embodied within it, and the way it is distributed and consumed.

How a Look Becomes Punk

Dress products presenting punk imagery have become commercialized and widely distributed, although that does not necessarily strip them of all punk value. The de-sign symbolism in punk style is affected by culture, fashion consumption, and prod-uct diffusion. Judy Attfield (2000) clarifies that the entirety of an object is more than its tactile and visible features, and also more than the social themes and ideas repre-sented in the look of its design. The complete narrative is within the object-subject relationship, where the wearer, viewer, and object all intertwine. With punk style this can be complicated when it comes to how it is produced and consumed because the garments often come from varied sources and are reconfigured physically and then overlaid with new meanings. Interpretations of the same garment can change based on the wearer and can transform throughout the diffusion cycle as the item is adopted for wider use.

Through whatever means the style is accepted into the punk aesthetic, part of its designation as punk can be traced back before it was acquired by the masses, to the source of the item's creation. Each step in the process from idea to everyone wearing it has a relationship to the punkness of the style. These steps include how the garment design was influenced and developed, how it is made, how it is distributed, how it is put together and worn with other garments as well as proportion on the body, and the demographics of the wearer combined with his or her experiences.

One way to look at things is fairly generally. Items are deemed punk and ad-opted into the common aesthetic recognizable to others as punk. Garments and modifications such as studded belts, vibrantly dyed hair, and combat boots became iconically punk in the eyes of many viewers through various forms, and initially were developed as punk through many channels. These channels include scene leaders, societal shifts such as politics and globalization, and fashion trends within the subculture and the mainstream. Another source of punk style is individual creative exploration within fashion and the personalization of one's style, as much of punk style is related to artistic desires and design.

The Influence of Scene Leaders

A person who influences punk style may be someone who is in a band, runs a zine, a record label, or a blog, organizes events, or is a fixture in the community. These highly visible members of the subculture have views that are respected and/or a personal style that appears practical and appealing to others. Naturally, witnesses and admirers adopt aspects of a leader's look. The person may be innovating through function, creativity, or necessity (such as distressed clothes), and he or she may or may not acknowledge their innovation at the time as style leaders. It may come over time through the incorporation of styles into a scene.

Designer Influence

Style can be birthed out of a designer's creativity. That individual may be considered a high fashion designer, such as Vivienne Westwood, Zandra Rhodes, or Anna Sui. Alternately a fashion-forward boutique, an up-and-coming designer, or a person with strong originality and flair can present looks that are the next big thing in punk. In the case of Westwood, her initial designs and the ideas of the punk movement were interwoven with ideology and visual manifestation going hand in hand. T-shirts with rips and redesigned through reshaping, painting over, and even running toy trucks over them were in part a functional response to an overload of a product. In 1972, there was a rock and roll revival show appealing to the Teddy Boy subculture that took place at Wembley Stadium. Westwood and McLaren made T-shirts that sported the Vive Le Rock! phrase to sell to this huge audience, but unfortunately did not sell any. This huge overstock laid the path for ideas about distressed clothes, as McLaren and Westwood had to do something with all that material. Roger explained:

> These T-shirts became the sort of palette. They distressed them, they dyed them, they ripped them, they did whatever ... they got their son Joe to run his little toy tractor over it. So there was a lot of attitude going on there. And really, I think Malcolm and Vivienne, of course they opened up in the back of Paradise Garage doing their '50s stuff, their Teddy Boy stuff ... that to me was a bit art school, a bit kind of like coming at it literally. But once they'd gotten over that and they started to mix it up a bit into Too Fast to

Live Too Young to Die with the rocker stuff, then it started to get a bit more interesting because they were having to distress stuff and probably more by, because they had to … to get rid of all these fucking T-shirts. (Interview with author, 2009)

Some of the original designs were conceived out of the DIY manner of working with available resources merged with creative passion of a designer.

Fig. 4.1 Vive Le Rock! shirt (copyright the Contemporary Wardrobe Collection, photograph Roger K. Burton).

Function

Necessity often drives invention, and many punks find their wardrobe is a construction of useful tools for a day's tasks. The crusty punk look is an example of style birthed out of function, but that has grown beyond that origin. It is aligned with lack of budget but also reflects ideas of hygiene, beauty, color palette, and design

preferences that differ from the norms of society. They are not always of low economic strata necessitating wearing the same boots duct taped together daily, but it is
a choice of how to have a relationship with one's clothes, and how dress is part of
an overall identity.

Creativity

Everyday individuals perform tasks to be a designer of sorts, by constructing their
appearance for daily life, and sometimes, the influence from self-creations can be
strong and lasting. This sort of design is not only relegated to those with the goal of
being an eye-catching fashion plate. It can be someone who finds a comfortable new
way to dress for skateboarding, an effective method to keep hair color lasting longer,
or an aging punk who reinvigorates old clothes through reshaping the fit or repurposing them as patches or baby onesies. Their fresh way of looking at the relationships
of objects to the body and objects to one another can strike a chord with viewers
who take the cue and want to make portions of the look their own. Often this will be
because the wearer has touched on an idea that resonates with the viewers as witty,
timely, and/or functional for their context.

Making Is Power: Power Is Negotiated

One way garments earn the punk moniker is the manner in which the garments were
physically created, including the process from fiber to fabric to garment to consumer.
They can be produced through fashion designers, such as Westwood and Japanese
deconstructionists Yohji Yamamoto and Rei Kawakubo. Punk can be developed on
the street via necessity, such as naturally ripped items not replaced because of a low
budget, through musicians whose identity is borrowed by fans to signify allegiance,
through groups that develop coded cues of communications, and through personalization. One can buy punk styles at stores or whip them up from scratch—and
everything in between by putting existing design elements together in specific ways.

For high fashion the production is not dissimilar to that of DIY or punk construction mixing independently designed and produced garments with premade items
configured in a new way. This does not make high fashion automatically punk, as
it rarely is, but it does illustrate similarities in some concepts and demonstrate that
punk and high fashion are not necessarily mutually exclusive, depending on the mes-
saging and motivations behind the design. For mass-market fashion, the production
differs greatly, as it is generally factory produced, with few unique qualities per garment, and reproduced in large quantities. While this does not make any of these items
punk, those details can affect whether an item will be embraced by punks.

There is a great deal of overlap between the punk subculture and the participants
in the resurgence of crafting. This is true not only of the DIY spirit, but also the

iconography used, the function of the items, and how they are worn and distributed. Modern crafters frequently incorporate a punk perspective into their knitting, sewing, and silk screening, all indicating that the creative outlet and ability to express oneself through dress are fundamental purposes in developing a punk style.

The creation of punk garments often lives between the worlds of couture and common, as mass-produced items are frequently reconfigured and repurposed. Punk fashion production is not always about actually starting from scratch, but about constructing a look, with variation in how the products are sourced. Danielle explained her enjoyment of developing her own style:

> For my punk dress, it is really different styles of clothing that you really don't see a lot. I really like to get one-of-a-kind things, or make them one-of-a-kind. I'll buy a shirt and add my own embellishments on it. Just to make it different … so you kind of have to look twice.

Different factions of punk have specific politics about how an item is made and what they will qualify as authentic and on topic with the social codes of that subgenre. These can include aspects such as brand name associations, textile choices, acceptable prices to pay, and where the item can be purchased.

Punk ensembles are often developed through DIY techniques, whether creating a garment from scratch, reinterpreting the old, or carefully selecting the manner in which ready-made things are worn. All of these options combine ideas from art and design, fashion and function. Making an item for oneself is a powerful thing and implants the meaning of that process upon the garments. This handcrafted or personally selected concept can be associated with punk. But power is negotiated, and the viewers of the clothing have a say as well in how they interpret it. The artisan and the viewer negotiate the worth of a garment together. The viewer can be the wearer himself, or an observer. Complications arise because a maker or wearer can have one intention regarding how the item is punk, and yet another viewer can read another intent as the message.

There is room for singular agenda as well as postmodern multiplicity. Some would assert that postmodernism's validation of multiple views of a garment negates the artisan or individual who develops his or her own style (Doy 2000). It devalues a finite message. However, this argument does not exactly apply to punk as there is a balance happening between individual production or wearing and consumer interpretation. Thus punk style can exist with sincerity and lack of sincerity both on the back of a basement show-going youth alongside his completely mainstream, football-focused classmate, depending on the wearer's intention.

Punk dress is a vehicle to make art, voice commentary, and revamp traditions for social change, all as part of everyday life. Therefore the production and embodiment of the garments will differ when worn by someone from a punk perspective versus someone who dons the attire with differing intentions.

Consequently, the interpretation can be based on how the producer is perceived. There are considerations about the punkness of a garment or look regarding the inclusion of heavy-handed marketing such as strong branding, which may have the wearer positioned as a representative for a company. To a viewer, that corporation's message becomes intertwined with the wearer's identity. This can have negative connotations, such as items appearing as inauthentic punk or those made by companies with known ties to labor injustice or linked to an aspect of mainstream culture that is quite distanced from subculture. Alternately, being linked to a corporation can provide the opposite effect if the branding is aligned with the punk lifestyle and represents that through its employees, the aesthetic, and marketing. A few examples the interviewees discussed were Vans, Converse, and Dr. Martens. Related, an individual's visual expression of identity can become its own sort of brand, with instant recognition from viewers, if the person perpetually creates a distinct style he or she becomes known for.

There is a vast sense of personal accomplishment when something is made with one's own hands, or a when single special item is found in a flea market or in an otherwise bland mall trip. The object is improved upon (in a punk sense) through personalization, time, wear, and embodiment. Danielle commented, "I think I'm more inventive now with my clothing than I was when I was younger with punk rock. Because I would just buy things that were punk rock, and now I'm making things that I know are punk rock to me."

The Humanity in DIY

In today's technologically dependent, hyper-automated era, a sense of autonomy can be lost. Therefore punk style can diminish negative feeling associated with restraint when one feels they are not being passive regarding their dress, but instead asserting control. Contemporary society's dependence on and fondness for computing, in particular the wealth of knowledge, social interaction, and entertainment, has high value, especially for a subculture built on those exact notions. Punk style and related DIY concepts represent a rebellion against that sense of lacking humanity, whether it is in making one's own items, fashioning one's own styles to suit one's unique vision, or simply wearing attire that represents independence from dogmatic groupthink of mainstream trends.

Through the DIY method, one validates the unusual or the unique, and also promotes the new or pays tribute to the potentially forgotten. Members of the subculture generally make the iconic items, such as one-inch buttons, patches, and T-shirts emblazoned with the names of bands, zines, and local scenes, although some of the older references, such as band logos from the biggest bands of the 1970s, are occasionally mass produced. Often products cannot be easily found in mainstream channels such as department stores or local chain stores. These little art pieces are worn as proud proclamations of an experience, and the semiotic markers serve as validation of one's involvement in the community and knowing personal interests.

This much attention to technology has created a backlash. While a reaction to the technological era may be relevant mostly to the latter-day punk motivations, it is not unrelated to the goal of earlier punks to express a message of personal or political meaning through their attire. Those reasons are now simply heightened when voices are lost in the din of endless binary. Also, as the twentieth century moved to a more machine-focused culture and jobs were lost (and others created) and everything automated, some felt their highly technologically based existence created a loss of individual identity combined with the stress of the fast pace of a multitasking culture. There are also social components to having attire that is personal and requires conversation; the act of constructing a look can also be relaxing and provide a creative outlet for its wearers or for a wearer for a who purchases it from a known creator and helps bring it back to life and away from automation. It makes the wearer feel less like an automaton.

A punk style is most effective when the developer of the look is a punk. Some of the meaning is dulled in the mass application of punk themes in mainstream-marketed, punk-appearing garments. Mass duplication, made on assembly lines and with no personalization, is a punk style representation of this antithesis. However, as previously discussed, punk style is so reliant on bricolage that all included items in a look can be mass produced, but it is the thoughtful choices in how they are woven together that makes the styling punk.

Colin Campbell continues this thread in describing the links between hand and machine:

> The contrast is not really between hand production and machine production, but rather between a production system in which the worker is in control of the machine and one in which the machine is in control of the worker ... one of the intriguing features of modern consumer society is the way in which machines have become reappropriated by the craft tradition, aiding and abetting craft products' consumers rather than robbing them of their traditional autonomy. What is significant ... is the fact that the human is in charge of the machine and not the machine of the human. (2005: 28)

While the sewing machine is a clear use of this concept, the Internet is also fundamental as part of modern DIY production, in learning about processes, promoting product, and developing community through shared interests.

Finding that equilibrium between the digital and the tangible worlds is a challenge, but one that punks are negotiating fairly successfully. Making one's own products is a way to turn the distant into the near and gain a sense of control and rarity in a world of automation and sameness. Punks do not reject new technology (Busch 2001). In fact, they often embrace it as a tool for knowledge, social connection, and disseminating ideas. It is also a location in which the DIY spirit regarding style can shine on commerce sites such as Etsy, Threadless, and Café Press, which feature individually made items and options such as numerous typefaces and how-to videos as well as user content creation in blogs, video podcasts, and video games. Punks prefer to make things themselves, and/or to feel their premade items do represent their ideas. The Web and new technologies speed up recognition and accessibility, so it is a merger of high and low tech, personal and mechanical. This is how items can be sold on Etsy, designed using the latest software, or purchased from mass-market mall stores but then personalized through the aesthetics of styling color, line, texture, and combination and still register as punk.

Another conflict in this technological era of human-machine interaction is the perceived high level of expertise needed to perform in the mechanized, digitized environment. Punks have long acknowledged their ability to independently or casually learn the proficiency needed, historically through the music they have played, the way zines were created, and even in the way punk fashion styles emerged. Masterful skill is not necessary to accomplish tasks or gain positive outcomes from participation.

The modern craft movement, highly aligned with punk styling and punks themselves, has many books and websites advocating this notion. One of the motivations for individuals to use a DIY method is that it does not always require a vast skill set. There is accessibility to this base-level DIY—anyone can give it a try. The grungy

Fig. 4.2 Handmade pin purchased at DIY craft fair, circa 2007 (copyright Monica Sklar and Harlo Petoskey).

imperfection that has cachet in punk style supports a novice crafter. This is a resurgence of thoughts that had not existed significantly since before the Industrial Revolution (Nicolay 2006; Woodcock 2006). What is referred to as DIY in underground Western culture is actually a global norm and a historical skill set, and it can function within or alongside the digitized world. In punk this is especially acceptable as perfection is rarely the aesthetic ideal, with deconstruction (including sometimes purposefully so) as the preferred styling, and therefore people are more willing to attempt to make their own jewelry or repair boots.

Merchandising Punk Style

There is merchandising *within* punk style and merchandising *of* punk style. They are inherently interwoven concepts even though at times there can be conflict. Punks need to obtain items that they can wear and feel they represent a punk attitude. Punk style is also utilized as a design feature in items merchandised to others. There is merchandising within punk, which is how punks learn about the styles and acquire them. There can be confusion and overlap between the two. There is confusion between merchandising within punk and merchandising of punk, as punks always remake objects but struggle when their objects are themselves reconfigured. They are not as formally split as they may appear, though, as ideas blend together, starting with Vivienne Westwood in the 1970s and the cornerstone ideas of appropriation and bricolage.

Punk style does not come out of thin air. The styles are learned about, then developed through DIY construction, purchasing, how items are worn together, and how ideas are marketed within the scene and outside the scene to others. Within the scene it is not so much blatant marketing as it is community ideas represented visually, usually first by one person, band, or regional style that then takes off, and those cues represent those ideas often for a long life cycle. There are trends within punk, such as baggy jeans or vintage sweater vests, that have life cycles not radically different from the mainstream in that they are introduced by style leaders and innovators (often bands), many adopt them, then they seem passé, and eventually something new is introduced. However some things within punk stay as having such a relationship to the band or concept that they were related to, or even the geography that they were derived from, that they endure because they were partially created out of function and partially in that reverence for honoring those who came before that is so pertinent to punk. Hebdige discussed this when he said that not all punks "were equally aware of the disjunction between experience and signification upon which the whole style is originally based. The style no doubt made sense for the first wave of self-conscious innovators at a level which remains inaccessible to those who became punks after the subculture had surfaced and became publicized" (1979: 122). With homage the symbolism within a garment can be maintained across generations. Future wearers start to embrace the style as representative of the spirit of previous wearers, yet not necessarily the reasons the original wearers chose that specific look.

The Diffusion of Punk Style

There are several views on exactly how style moves through society (Kawamura 2005), whether it shifts from the elite to the masses (McCracken 1988; Simmel 1904; Veblen 1899), or via the numerous routes of collective selection of individuals choosing together among the variety of styles (Blumer 1969), eventually leading to a style making its way from an innovator with a new idea to a mass norm to an overused concept only worn by laggards and then back around to innovation again (Sproles 1979).

Whichever route through the particular segments of society a style takes, it moves through a process of diffusion from where the idea started outward to everyone. Rogers defines diffusion as "the process by which an innovation is communicated through certain channels over time among the members of a social system" (2003: 5). His description of the process contains four primary elements: innovation, communication channels, time, and a social system (2003: 36–37).

The social structure of the punk subculture, with its network of personalities, internal media sources, and production and consumption tools, combined with its long-term resilience versus a brief trend, gives it the tools to have multiple styles at different points of the cycle of adoption all at the same time. There can be things that are innovated, worn because they are classic, and that are commonplace simultaneously, and these all serve different purposes within the scene, and outside of it when worn by mainstream wearers.

Style changes can reflect the influence of a fashion leader, a regional or cultural shift, or a subgenre within the overall subculture. With that there is a cycle during which these looks are invented, brought into punk, then arrive into subcultures beyond punk. There are fashion cycles within the subculture, yet individuality is valued and allowed to play perhaps a larger role than within mainstream fashion cycles. That individuality constantly tweaks the cycle from being a routine rehash of the same garments worn the same way. However, individuality is in fact part of the fashion cycle as innovation by someone and then adoption by others is essential to keep the cycle moving. Punk style can have variations on the cycle because aspects of its fashion can be brief or lasting and differ dramatically in form. Also there can be differing interpretations from inside and outside of the subculture as to what constitutes authentic punk style, and so where a garment is positioned on the cycle can be subject to perspective.

Sproles (1974) described the steps of the diffusion process and how clothing shifts from one group to the next. Within the diffusion process, individuals pick up on punk stylistic ideas and start dressing that way at their own pace, which occurs at different rates of adoption (Rogers 2003). Five adopter categories serve as a classification system of people on the basis of their innovativeness. The categories are innovators, early adopters or opinion leaders, the early majority or masses, the late majority and more of the masses, and laggards (Rogers 2003; Sproles 1974).

On a typical chart of fashion cycles, the punks are to the side of innovators and early adopters, with the mainstream then adopting those looks and laggards making them tired. New innovations within punk then take hold and it all starts over again. Fashion leaders are also those within punk who innovate styles that others copy, or those who represent a segment of the culture because they lead a popular band or scene. Augie explains this phenomenon:

> I used to look at records and see what so-and-so was wearing. And that would be a model for what I would wear. And it was kind of like a go-to; well I can wear this because Ian from Minor Threat wore it. Henry from Black Flag wore it. You study things under a magnifying glass and all the minutia you pick up on and then you end up being a carbon copy if someone else did it first. So, then that evolved, as I wanted to not be just a carbon copy of everything that came before me.

With this he explains how punk style often evolves into its next ideation by an individual employing his or her personal take and functional needs onto a previous style.

When a style moves from the innovator to a select crowd, they are the early adopters. Peterson said:

> A lot of hardcore kids were drawn to the music via skateboarding so it's natural that the "skater" look would be an influence. The beads came from the Krishna influence in the scene—particularly after the rise of [bands] Shelter and 108. It's not that these bands told people to wear these items. Rather, they wore them and people were curious about the ideas and, I feel, subconsciously started to wear some of the items. (Interview with author, 2011)

As things move into mass and late adoption, it may be a celebrity, an alternative band that crosses over, product designs from a mainstream store, or an admired designer who reproduced the items. This process and the interpretation of it depends on whether punk style is viewed as related to an ideology or as a style innovation in the cycle of adoption through society. It is probably a little of both; thus, it is lasting styles, such as mohawks, and it is fluctuating trends, such as skinny or baggy jeans, within the subgenres. In our efforts to be individual and different, those within the mainstream might adopt some choices from an outsider culture. The "look at me" era of reality TV and aspects of social networking affect this notion. Punks also incorporate themselves into the mainstream through the style being around so many decades and through their own willingness to blend styles within subculture, as well as to merge subculture and mainstream styles to suit not only their taste but, when necessary, to better fit into their environment.

As the style moves into all facets of consumption and distribution, it often strains to maintain its cachet with the original wearers, who may still don the look or may have adjusted it to provide new distinction from the norm wearing it. Punk, with its emphasis on history but also on the future and against the status quo, goes through a process of complete reinvention along with refreshing previous concepts and keeping some in time capsule form out of respect for the scene's lineage.

Routes to Obtain Punk Style

Punk styles achieve their diffusion through various distribution channels. Each method of transferring the product to the consumer leaves its own imprint and changes the garment's relationship to punk. One way to obtain punk items is from

Fig. 4.3 Independently produced and distributed items at an anarchist book fair in San Francisco, California (copyright Grace Bartlett).

punks themselves who have made the wares, or to purchase otherwise independently made wares, often at "distro" tables at shows and events.

The rejection of current notions of consumerism has led to the creation of products for oneself, as well as the development of alternative items to bring to market and variance in promotional strategy. This is rarely where full garments or whole ensembles such as pants, sweaters, and shoes are acquired, but more so items that are easy and affordable to purchase wholesale and to duplicate logos on. T-shirts, patches, buttons, and similar general-use and small-scale items are easier for merchandisers to carry around in volume from show to show, simple for a consumer to pick up and hold on to in a bustling environment, and often represent something related to the event. Prices for items such as T-shirts in this independent marketplace are generally low as there is limited prioritization in profit margins, since motivations are driven primarily by the dissemination and expression of subcultural ideas.

Similarly, some body modifications, such as piercings or haircuts, have been performed in this intimate atmosphere. The nature of the one-on-one interaction with other punks brings a heightened level of punkness to the styling due to the very DIY nature of the context. Audra explained that the particulars of how she got her tongue pierced add to its validation as punk: "I think the angle it was done on and the fact that the jewelry was done by [a piercer within the Detroit punk community who pierced in his home and at punk events] makes it feel a little more punk I guess than someone who got it done on spring break."

Another route used to obtain punk styles is online sources. These range from independent producers using consolidated forums such as Etsy to large-scale producers of mass-marketed versions of punk styles using the Web. The Internet also brings accessibility to those punks who do not live in a community with bricks-and-mortar retailers of punk wares and/or that regularly features events where a punk might sell or give away goods. Auction sites such as eBay have made vintage and used punk wares more accessible. This traveling of goods keeps things alive that may have languished in donation bags and basements. The Internet also creates the ability to acquire items from around the globe and from any era, which can drive up prices of some pieces to meet the demands of limited-run items having lasting desirability. Prices online are wide ranging, from DIY producers who wish simply to cover their expenses and perhaps make just enough money to produce the next item, through vintage dealers who cash in on punk "celebrities" and the rareness of original punk wares that often did not survive the rough wear and tear, elevating prices to art auction levels, and even producing counterfeits to satisfy market demand and for pure exploitive profiteering.[1]

The plethora of blogs covering street style, mainstream, and high fashion do not play a large role in the distribution of punk fashion, as most punks are not die-hard fashion trend followers. However the ever-growing prominence of style blogs, of all types, does introduce ideas of appearance creation to those looking for creative inspiration. There are some alternative-style blogs, including those featuring the litany of styles considered punk. This can prove a resource for knowledge about historic styles, or for how-to tips on through the depth of knowledge available to reference on topics such as the mechanics of the garments/tools of steampunk, or the perfect way to pin curl a rockabilly or punk hairdo.

Some style blogs even go as far as to mock those who fall into the trap of being "hipsters," which is a term within subculture that can take on a negative connotation where the line between creative physical expression has somehow crossed into a territory that lacks sincerity or perceived analytical thought, and becomes a source of mocking for others.[2] However most websites and blogs featuring punk style are geared toward knowledge and admiration. Often it renews life to forgotten images of punks from the past and inspires new generations.

Small, generally independently owned boutiques are another source of acquiring punk styles. This includes everything from meticulously designed shops to record stores with a T-shirt section. These stores often feature the wares of independent designers both local and national (even global sometimes) and highlight small-run items. The prices are often higher than at the mall or through completely DIY channels in these stores, as one is paying for the labor of the worker, for the uniqueness of the design, and often for a designer or brand trying to grow into a business. Sometimes the prices are lower than mainstream ready-to-wear as the designer is unknown and there is no markup for the couture cachet of major branding. Many punks enjoy this environment for shopping, as it is unusual for the items to be seen on others and the shopping experience may include a social component as the environment or people within it may construct a punk context. Furthermore, the designers whose garments are featured in said stores often are part of the subcultural frame of reference and blend iconography appealing to the punk mindset and trends within alternative culture at any given time.

Early punk boutiques from the 1970s and 1980s featured clothing that appealed to consumers of punk style. Westwood and McLaren's various incarnations of the same storefront (Let It Rock/SEX/Seditionaries) in London were pivotal in bringing the style to the punks of that region. Similarly Manic Panic was an institution in New York. Snooky explained what it was like to open a boutique focused on punk at that time:

> Created by punks, for punks, it was very well received by both punks and the press, because it was the real deal—a one-of-a-kind. The old folks in the 'hood were a bit afraid of us at first, but then accepted us when they realized we were harmless. Soon other stores on the block started carrying punk style merchandise, and other punk boutiques opened. St Marks Place became [the] punk mecca in America!

Other important early punk shops included Trash and Vaudeville in New York, which was the first in the United States to distribute Dr. Martens, Acme Attractions in London, Poseur and NaNa in Los Angeles, Cat's Meow in multiple Midwest locations, and The Alley in Chicago (Roeck and Schottlaender 1999; Yeebo 2012).

Fig. 4.4 Tish and Snooky at the original Manic Panic store, New York City, 1970s (copyright Manic Panic, photographer Estelle Bellomo).

Fig. 4.5 Purple fishnet top purchased at Trash and Vaudville, New York City, 1990s (copyright Monica Sklar and Harlo Petoskey).

How the ensemble is put together and the way it is embodied by the wearer enables certain styles to evoke punk, regardless of the origins of the individual pieces that make up the look. Therefore buying punk attire through completely mainstream sources is tricky and requires subtle attention to detail on the part of the wearer. In this mid-priced market, one can buy all J.Crew, typically nonpunk styles but come across as punk through how the garments are combined and styled, such as layering techniques, color and pattern choices, the manner in which it is accessorized, and proportions. Denise described how she can shop at chain specialty and department stores, including discounters, and by taking items and creating her own styling she constructs a punk appearance.

This is contrasted against someone who buys a ready-made punk outfit with band names, plaids, vintage styling, and chunky accessories at a mall's chain store that attempts to cater to alternative lifestyles, and yet does not come across as sincerely punk. Kathy added:

It is almost like how someone carries themselves more than how they're actually dressed. Because I see a kid who looks like [mall chain store] Hot Topic's dream child walk around, you're like "that kid is not punk rock at all." And then you see another kid who's got on a studded belt and maybe tight jeans and a pair of creepers and just a regular T-shirt, and you're like "that's a punk rock kid."

Fig. 4.6 Contemporary woman's olive green jacket personalized with The Clash silk-screened patch (copyright Monica Sklar and Harlo Petoskey).

Designer apparel available via department stores, high-end boutiques, and the designers themselves generally does not fall under the punk umbrella, however it can. That which is styled to be distinctive and artistic is somewhat in line with original punk concepts, such as Westwood's lines, however designer apparel is frequently more accepted by punks when it exists outside of the punk realm, as the manner in which the punk subculture progressed meant it primarily moved away from the high-fashion influence. Additionally, the expense of such garments, as well as the elitism that can be attached to them symbolically can be conflicting notions for many punks.

A challenge can come in accepting the designs of those such as Anna Sui or Marc Jacobs, who assert a relationship to subculture and punk through their personal lives

Fig. 4.7 The way the clothes and dress details are put together and embodied can exhibit punk, 1984 (copyright Tanya Seeman, photographer Kyle Bradfield).

historically, and whose designs often do reflect aspects of punk style, but when the apparel crosses an invisible boundary from appreciator to imitator it can prove disastrous to the designer as a source of mocking or even sheer distaste on the part of the viewer punks.

The production, marketing, and distribution channels, combined with the wearer's knowledge and commitment to subculture take ready-to-wear clothes and swing them in one direction or the other. This is not to say that a chain mall store is ineffective at marketing punk wares, as some individuals do shop at those types of stores and successfully select and wear garments that reflect their punk interests with sincerity, just as some people who wear an all J.Crew outfit that is mismatched or ill-fitting do not come across as punk, but simply as poorly styled. Again, it is often in the wearer's presence (Brake 1985).

The mainstream market is where a punk internally debates his or her stance on mass-market production techniques and how they will employ punk politics when utilizing those goods. Some avoid that market altogether, attempting to circumvent the issue and not contribute to the problems such as labor issues, environmental challenges with waste through overproduction, and oppressive marketing that often employs negatively stereotypical references. Others use the manner in which the garments are styled to demonstrate punk political stances through ideas such as distorting the body shape intended by the designer by wearing the clothes larger or smaller than the norm, using trendy items in unconventional combinations, or conventional items such as formalwear or business attire as daily wear.

In addition to the mainstream stores' garments that can be configured to be punk, and the subcultural themed stores' garments that can read as punk or not, there is another equation in the mall stores, which is when punk iconography trends upward. There is a great deal of evidence of the diffusion of punk iconography through mainstream channels, however there was limited variation in its application and the types of stores it was found in. It goes in trends, and at times has reflected the influence of the Pacific Northwest's music scene or the 1980s bright colors and graffiti images. Blatant references to the 1970s punk styles, particularly the iconic look, do exist, and can be found in the commonality of pyramid studs on handbags, shoes, and belts, as well as typography that is cut-and-paste lettering and hand-painted graphics. Abstract leanings toward the punk aesthetic exist in mainstream styles through examples such as unusually placed zippers or garments with black with red or white stripes or tartan plaids. Some trends exist on many places of the fashion cycle simultaneously, and are accepted within punk and the mainstream in unison. The skull and crossbones graphic is one example, and while that image does evoke fear and negative overtones, making it a natural for punk, it was used on everything from baby onesies to adult T-shirts in the mainstream to dance with edginess in the most benign way. Punk styles are infrequently seen in retailers in mid through high price points aimed toward adult consumers, most likely because of the association of punk with youth, as well as the aesthetic challenges of incorporating the look into a multitasking, workplace wardrobe.

Often punk styles that have become mainstream trends succumb to over saturation and are discarded fairly quickly, therefore making it to mid- to low-priced markets briskly and staying there for a while. Mainstream stores featuring a punk aesthetic in their clothes commonly target a juniors market, with a modest price geared toward fast fashion and rapid trend acceptance and rejection. In addition to junior girls, another type of store that commonly carried punk-influenced attire was the high-volume chain stores catering to co-ed crowds in the teen to college-aged bracket. They are most likely aimed at early majority to late majority adopters. These stores are not so revolutionary that they are aimed toward innovators or early adopters, but their products are in the midst of the current styles, left of center, featuring mid-priced goods of moderate quality. Their clothes commonly feature guitars, silk-screened graphics, skull and crossbones, studded belts, skateboard shoes, and even some fairly overt likenesses of known punk personalities. These stores do cater to self-identified punks or alternative individuals as well as people who are not interested in punk, but are capturing the latest styles. Therefore the products are hard to classify as derivative or authentic, because the images are consistent, but it is the clientele buying them that would interpret the garments wholly differently: as the trend for this summer, or as lifestyle wear.

Mall stalwart Hot Topic, which opened its first store in 1988, features an array of punk-styled garments ranging from hair dyes to band T-shirts to black vinyl pants to leopard belts. Interpretations of Hot Topic's place in punk style are a subject of debate, as this store has been closely related to punk culture, but has been scrutinized as a location for a sanitized and commercialized version of punk. The design elements of dress products sold there often differ very little from those sold at independent boutiques, merchandise tables at punk shows, and Internet distributors. It seems the location of Hot Topic, within mall settings, as well as the inherent fact it is a chain store, is perhaps the most problematic aspect for some punk consumers. The nature of a chain store means mass produced and widely distributed, as well as an unknown recipient of the consumer's money, as compared to internal community, DIY, and distinct.

The term *mall punk* has emerged within the punk community as a snarky reference to Hot Topic shoppers and those who shop through similar outlets. The phrase indicates a notion of buying an image rather than living a lifestyle. Interesting, if a person shops at other mainstream mall stores, and puts the look together to create punk styling, for some punk viewers this is seen as more in line with punk's original notions than going to a chain punk boutique and buying the entire ensemble already pieced together. This is closely aligned with the discussions of fashion existing as a negative component of punk identity, rather than a sincerely expressive one, as some punks feel in the current marketplace it is simply too easy to don a front of punkness with one mall trip's purchases. It can be impossible to truly tell who has put their items together straight off the merchandising displays at Hot Topic, and who carefully crafted their day's attire from things collected through hard-fought experiences. However it is not uncommon for punks to feel they can discern a level of authenticity, even with similarly styled garments by the wearer's argot. This is where some of the detail-oriented aesthetics comes in, such as obscure band names, or an item being worn in through long-term usage, putting together whole looks from disparate styles, origins, and brands, and of course, whether the person wearing the attire can "talk the talk" on the subjects they are representing and/or is seen actively participating at scene events. It can be read as condescending that a person who purchases a shirt one place is less legitimate within punk than one who purchases a similar shirt at another venue, particularly when there is no structured definition of punk. This goes straight to the notion that punk style itself helps to create those definitions, and punks are looking for ways to push even their own boundaries, while acknowledge there are some parameters they happily function within to align themselves with something (and some people) they feel comfortable with.

Rejection of Mainstream Distribution Channels

Within punk there is some rejection of conventional contemporary consumerism. This can drive the flamboyantly dressed punk to embellish her own attire, the crusty punk to wear only a handful of items as his entire wardrobe, or the steampunk enthusiast to dive into history and fantasy for inspiration. Even the emo or hardcore punks, who may appear to be dressed in fairly conventional sportswear, often select brands and iconography quite carefully, frequently shop at used resellers, and focus on the subculture's guidelines for attractiveness rather than mainstream trends.

The empowerment of making one's own style rather than being a walking billboard from a ready-made trend or brand is motivated out of this notion. It may often reflect the personal economic situation of the punk as well. Many feel they have the right to enjoy fashion consumption, but its negative tone within punk chatter is generally reflected in a rejection of some of the morals perceived to accompany fashion production and consumption. Some punks cannot accept the methods with which many products are made, marketed, and distributed. Therefore, self-made and/ or sold items suit these consumers. The goals of this stance are often to support local economies as well as promote a separation from corporate dependence.

For punks this is rooted in personal economic situations and attitudes that reflect the times. Clothing can be an expensive component of one's budget, and therefore most punks do not want things that are disposable and they also do not want items that are too costly for their means. Yet there is awareness that low cost sometimes means workers who were not paid a fair wage and work in poor conditions, which is a conundrum for sociopolitically minded punks. In addition to issues of sustainability and affordability, being selective about attire is particularly relevant when dress is about combining ideas of identity commitment. There is also the notion in punk that the signs of use on a garment through long-term wear makes it more one's own, personalized with lifeblood ingrained in it. Stains, patches, wear lines, and rips are a material version of experiences. More often than not, though the crafter may purchase supplies from a craft store, he or she does not continue the sales chain in a traditional way. Similarly, when the punk purchases items from mainstream stores, he or she does not wear them in the exact manner they were shown in the store. Consequently, a radical consumer behavior of punks and related movements such as modern crafters is that they often reuse or remake items for themselves or to give away, therefore effectively eliminating the mainstream consumer/marketing equation. In current society's fashion cycle, that is highly unusual behavior and its progressive/back-to-roots combination could be assessed as antifashion.

One of the major motivating forces is a rejection of the current rampant consumerism that is perceived as negative by many punks. Campbell argues consumers have been seen in the past as two types of agents: "an active, calculating and rational actor, someone who carefully allocates scarce resources to the purchase of goods and services in such a manner as to maximize the utility obtained. The other, most often encountered in the writings of critics of 'the mass society,' is that of the passive, manipulated and exploited subject of market forces, someone who, as a consequence, is largely 'constrained' to consume in the way that they do" (2005: 23).

The punk consumer often falls into a third category of a more thoughtful consumer who developed in the postmodern era. This third consumer has emerged and continues to develop as one who carefully gathers goods with the plan to contentiously manipulate their symbolic meaning and express identity and lifestyle (Campbell 2005). This stance has informed the alternative take on clothing, such as in the DIY traditions, and is a continuation of the countercultural attitudinal developments of the mid-to-late twentieth century.

For some the production of punk attire maintains the same motivations as previous generations of punks, including personal economics and reactions against mainstream consumerism. However for a select group, it has grown to include a next step in this process and has surpassed the "No Logo" concept (Klein 1999) regarding the desire not to present corporate branding as a form of free advertising and a visual and monetary show of support for corporations' ideals. This new consumer, in the punk spirit, moves in a direction less oppressed and reactionary and more toward personal agency and accomplishment with an attitude indicating he or she would rather advertise "my logo" (Mutanen 2007) as compared to no logo or a brand's signifier emblazoned across one's chest.

The goal of this type of punk consumer is to "subvert conventional fashion … put your own individual mark on the clothes you wear" and explore options beyond those encouraged and available through mass market fashion systems (Rannels, Alvarado, and Meng 2006).

This is not to say they make every product they wear, as they do not. Sometimes there is self-creation of the items, but more so it is that "how you wear it" stamp of punkness through creative identity expression that exudes "my logo." This is delicate alongside the pride and kinship-building use of wearing the iconography of brands long associated with punk. However that is again where punk is vastly postmodern in that it can have multiple accurate messages coexisting.

Gender Issues and Politics through Punk Production and Consumption

Handmade items can be a form of identity expression and a tactile manifestation of sociopolitical opinions. Politics are an extremely powerful motivating factor for the reemergence of craft with discussion of using fair trade materials and an awareness of the connection between some punk ideals, such as anarchist movements, labor issues, and environmentalism. Making one's own clothing and/or being a very conscientious consumer of clothing bought through mainstream channels, including having it styled to suit the individual, are ways in which individuals can take a level of control on a very personal level over enormous political, social, and environmental issues about which individuals often feel overwhelmed and lacking power. Daily dress choices, including how the garments are manufactured, obtained, and worn, can be a form of resistance (Railla 2007).

In addition to punk style addressing the role of political thought as enacted in daily experience, it also addresses gender issues. Creating a style dubbed punk accepts a certain amount of discussion about gender in society. Fashion and sincere enthusiasm for dress is generally perceived as inherently feminine, which contrasts the masculine engendered unpinning commonly aligned with punk. Yet the act of making one's own attire, or self-styling rather than full-throttle buying into what has been marketed to you, is considered punk. This is particularly true in the United States, where effortless cool reigns as the demeanor as compared to some other cultures where effort marks commitment and reflects depth of character within that nation's subcultural scene. When punks are raging against fashion, they are not raging against a person having some interest in clothing and visual presentation, as it is agreed that one's dress expresses identity and has functionality. Rather, their passionate distaste is against the perception that grooming and adornment are feminine and therefore "weak." This perception of fashion is exacerbated by the passivity of allowing oneself to be a follower, especially in the manner of being a patsy for corporate marketing or mainstream trends, and therefore also weak, as compared to punk's "anti-" stance.

The initial feminist movements of the twentieth century generally disregarded craft as it was seen as solely women's work and therefore constricting. However, new, post-Riot Grrrl and postmodern feminists are embracing craft and repositioning the argument (Stoller 2003; Woodcock 2006). Stoller (2003) sees it as antifeminist that only activities historically viewed as male are worthwhile for continuation. Male inclusion in craft DIY is on the rise, although with much of the current motivation being a reevaluation of feminist ideologies of women's work, it is not surprising that male participation is limited and often relegated to particular mediums, forms, and styles. However, based on the variety of political and social motivations pushing the movement, it could be expected that male presence will quickly increase and vary.

Men in punk do make their own things, but often it is not aligned with a feminist stance or the history of women's roles in society; thus there remains a masculine imprint on their tasks as physical and hard materials, rather than aligning them with the feminine lineage. The duct tape to wrap boots, the stamping in of metal studs, the mechanized one-inch button press, and the highly physical act of silk screening, may be deemed masculine forms of DIY, regardless of the obvious stereotyping and reinforcement of gender roles. There are facets of punk subgenres that have men who openly embrace femininity and named feminism, yet that does not necessarily carry over to all who self-identify as punk or who derive interpretations of the different types of DIY punk style creation. In subculture there is ebb and flow of this notion over time. Extreme examples would be periods of hardcore that embraced ready-made sportswear more so than individual or flashier fashions, reflecting the dominance of masculine men during the time period. This was as compared to Riot Grrrls with their re-envisioning of vintage clothes, and the body modification norms of writing on oneself to completely personalize dress.

A theme in writings on dress is to review the higher value assessment placed on historically men's gendered activities over historically women's activities. This carries over to the physical proportions of self-made or self-styled products. An outfit someone has carefully created or a patch they have meticulously sewn on are quiet broadcasts of politics as compared to the (often) growling and screaming male fronting of an equally loud punk band on an (often) elevated stage. Whether the wearer of said styles is male or female is secondary to the notion that the loud can overshadow the quiet, the big presence the small. Fashion items are intimate; one often has to see them up close to recognize the details. Ramlijak reinforced this when she said: "There is a long-standing bias in our culture toward largeness over smaller, more intimate things. In simplified terms the cultural equation goes as follows: Big/male/public versus small/female/private" (2004: 186–95).

The Results of Punk Style Traveling through Fashion Channels

The abundance of Ramones items filling retail stores around the country is one highly visible example of the presence of punk dress in the mainstream. The Rock and Roll Hall of Fame inductees formed in New York City in 1974 and continued to put out albums and tour until 1996. Their signature eagle insignia and the simple block-font logo of their name have become common retail fare, even more so than their music. While they never had significant record sales, they have sold 1.5 million T-shirts since their 1996 breakup, and the death of lead singer Joey immediately prompted a leading teen clothing retailer to order 10,000 Ramones T-shirts (Browne 2008).

Manic Panic is another remnant of 1970s New York City punk that has become a large part of modern consumption. Co-founder Snooky said:

> Punk style stores started popping up all over the country. They all wanted to carry the same products as us, so we started to wholesale our best-selling items to them ... It was all very organic—we learned every aspect of the biz by just doing it ... By the time our lease was up and the rent was quadrupling in 1989, our wholesale business was booming. So we gave up our original storefront and for the next several years concentrated mainly on wholesale. (Interview with author, 2012)

Manic Panic's signature product is hair dye, and the brand revolutionized the conventional coif, making it easy to have shades of blue, green, purple, and bright red. Business acumen turned an underground punk look into a forty-year business aimed

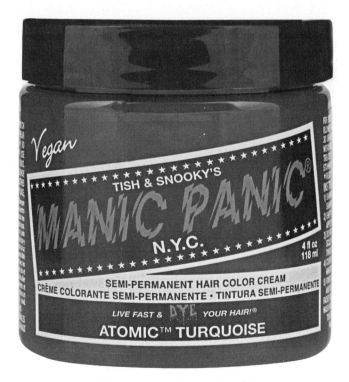

Fig. 4.8 Manic Panic hair dye (copyright Manic Panic).

toward punkers and the masses alike, with products sold around the globe at millions in annual revenues. As their business has grown, their attempts to maintain a connection to punk ideals has not changed. Snooky said, "Even though Manic Panic has grown over the years to the iconic brand it is today, while keeping professional, we still maintain a very DIY punk attitude and approach to everything we do" (Interview with author, 2012).

As the umbrella of punk widens and the subculture matures over time, there is a need for the individuals and businesses within it to navigate how to retain a punk ideology while interacting with mainstream society. Punk style has integrated itself into every aspect of fashion. While maintaining its original cachet with subcultural wearers, the aesthetic is also seen on high-fashion runways, in mainstream mall stores, and in every ideation imaginable on the street as part of daily wear for legions of youth, hipsters, and anyone who came of age during or after punk regardless of subcultural leaning. It has taken in influences from each of those facets of society, and has provided stylistic markers that have become ingrained into the numerous types of fashion cycles affecting a wide swath of consumers.

Punk Style and Its Relationship to Street Style

Punk style has a very close relationship with the street style of youth (predominately) but also people of all ages around the globe. Punk emerged as an expression of art, politics, and individuality, which are also common themes driving street style choices. Street style and subcultural style intersect but are not necessarily one and the same. Subcultural style and street fashion are often overlapping, and sometimes confused, but they are different. Subcultural style leans more toward group participation in a larger body of information or a movement related to some form of identity formation, such as punk, goth, ska, skater, and so forth. Subcultural style can be created by designers, style leaders within a community, individual wearers, and groups of people, such as youth involved in a subculture. Street style is individually based, although it embraces trends, movements, communities, and high fashion, but is rooted in one individual's take on how to spin that into his or her image. This is not to say that street style does not have groupings and commonalities within it, rather that it is a form of daily wear and reflects a merged usage of all of the fashions available, rather than a mall's mannequins, a runway's couture, or a subculture's uniform. Street style takes all of that and spins it for function and personality. In addition to influencing street styles that have come after it, punk style is also influenced *by* street styles.

Fashion and lifestyle issues such as having a low budget influenced using and remaking old garments and wearing items that are ripped, safety pinned together, and showing stains and wear. Another example may be items in large or small proportions to the body, which has an aesthetic purpose of reconfiguring body image but also gives the appearance that things are just grabbed for preference and used by others as vintage and hand-me-downs.

In the United Kingdom, fashion designers with countercultural points of view developed much of what would become iconic punk style. In the United States, much of what became punk style was developed as functional street fashion for an individual or a region, and then became synonymous with the band wearing it, or a leader within the scene that people emulated the spirit of. Seattle's aesthetic of the 1990s, dubbed grunge, was a noteworthy example of this. The climate and cultural conditions of the Pacific Northwest made it highly practical to dress in flannel shirts, long underwear, rugged boots, and blue jeans. Through diffusion cycles, those garments and that style became fashion staples of counterculture throughout the country for a brief time.

Punk Style and Its Relationship to High Fashion

On the other end of the spectrum from street style, punk style is also heavily related to high fashion and its designer runways. There is an overlap to aspects of punk style and high fashion even though it is sometimes begrudgingly admitted to from the punk side. The products are of limited run, often manufactured by craftspeople, with a designer's characteristic stamp and an air of exclusivity. Punk style has a not entirely dissimilar relationship to high fashion; it influences it and has at times been influenced by it. Some inside the punk scene scoff at those they dub fashion punks. This is a critique at anyone wearing the style that does not embody it with sincerity, but also refers to the lineage of designers Westwood and McLaren who would dress the Sex Pistols and others in their wares. This is not to say everyone wearing it was a shill or that it was created as a big marketing scene. Westwood and McLaren helped shape the antiauthoritarian commentary and visual aesthetic that would become part of punk's framework. Wearers were not solely advertisement but were spreading broader messages. For many initial punks, particularly in the London scene, wearing the fashions was the punk part, it was the way to stand out, spread a message of revolt, and mess with mainstream society; the affiliated music came later (Marco, Interview with author, 2009). This general concept has lived on through every ideation of punk, whether the wearer or a designer creates it.

A second tactic sees designers adopt punk styles into their looks, which has received a mixed response from those in and out of the subculture. Some do in fact adopt it and strip it of all initial meaning and intention, thus recreating it in their own image, as high fashion or mass fashion design, within new intensions of art or commerce or simply pleasing aesthetics when the punk style has become de rigueur. Punks frequently do not appreciate that form of appropriation. When a designer uses punk-inspired style aesthetics in runway or mainstream designs, they do claim interest or appreciation of punk. This is a middle ground, which some punks appreciate as an artistic or high-end version of their clothes, and others find offensive and exploitive. The details seem to be the key, whether the brand or designer is seen as ingrained in or related to the punk subculture, or whether the person is completely outside.

Designer Anna Sui, who was a participant during some of the first waves of punk in the 1970s and 1980s, refers to the unwritten code of black, white, red and patterns such as leopard print and stars that were accepted or even prescribed. Her personal style and professional output have been influenced by the parameters of punk style (Nika 2011). This is true of many designers, yet when Marc Jacobs and Anna Sui did collections inspired by 1990s alternative styles they were lambasted by punks as interlopers. Yet they claim allegiance to alternative lifestyles and were present in many punk or subcultural affairs; they just chose to present their designs to a higher-end market. The designers developed collections influenced by genres aligned with the punk subculture but say they were in some manner a part of those cultures, attending music events and engaging with some of the community such as the musicians. They feel they understood the messages of the clothes when they took them into a new sphere.

Is it the way they are marketed, on the backs of rail-thin runway models, in the pages of *Vogue,* and priced out of reach of the punks that inspired them that brings out the ire? When Westwood designed for punks, had them wear it, and sold it right to them, it was slightly different to modern-day designers doing that and skipping the punk customer base. The designers and brands that are more middle market or mainstream find themselves in similar situations, in that they may be embracing punk's aesthetics—the skull and crossbones, the leopard print—but whether it is seen as exploitation or a growth of the style depends on whether they include punk's customer base in a way that reads as sincere.

Dress Up and Dress Down in Punk Style

Punk's relationship to street style and high fashion manipulates the outlook on dress up versus dress down modes of fashion. The differences in London and New York styles, as well as the subgenres that follow, often fall along the lines of a dress up versus dress down debate about the core punk looks. Punk styles are often at the forefront of upcoming trends in wider culture. Punk culture exists as a critique of the status quo, and the sociopolitical overtones that drive the fashion choices from a punk "more extreme" perspective may make their way into broader acceptance as that sentiment about culture is normalized. The resulting dress behaviors then make their way across culture, although through the diffusion channels some of the original ideas can be lost, and punks then start again developing ways to visually represent their ideas.

Dress up and dress down come in and out of favor even within subcultures, including within punk (Polhemus 1994). The highly elaborate British-inspired looks with the plaid bondage pants, tall boots, multicolored hair, and shiny metal everywhere can be seen as a form of dressing up. The aptly named "crusty" or "gutter punk" version of this attire, however, when mostly worn in black colors and unwashed, would be considered dressed down thematically, even if it is almost equally elaborate in its accessorizing and detail orientation. The New York scene, while stylish and creative, emphasized dress-down styles that were more function than fashion and that evolved into the skateboard, emo, and hardcore styles utilizing athletic wear, blue jeans, and T-shirts as common items. Hardcore and emo scenes typically are dressed down in their aesthetic. This variation has made its way into the mass knowledge and shaped fashion at times to shift toward presenting a polished or disheveled appearance and everything in between.

An intersection of dress up and dress down is the deconstruction movement in high fashion, especially the 1980s Japanese visionary designers Yohji Yamamoto and Rei Kawakubo and their avant-garde garments with unfamiliar shapes, frayed edges, exposed seams, and purposeful disproportions. The styles reflected the complications of life and the potential of artistic output. This would cycle into the mainstream as trends of distressed denim come and go, to the point where items are sold pre-ripped or wearers use files and bleach to break down the fibers before a single wearing. In this case, it is the dress up of the high fashion designers that is more closely aligned with general punk ideals or artistic vision and social commentary through appearance, while the mass-market trend version cuts to the finish line with no experience along the way.

Dress up and dress down is complicated by the punk concept that there is value in the experience of acquiring and wearing an item and that it shows in the level of distress an item has. Thus a punk often uses an item such as a T-shirt, a leather jacket, or boots for many years, breaking them in, adding patches and writing, rips and stains, and with each sign of use showing commitment and longevity to punk. This is demonstrated in the items of the dress up version of punk style, such as well-worn leather accessories. This has participated in the motivating factors behind the resurgence, especially in high-end menswear, of heritage brands, those that have been around since the early twentieth century, and the idea of a man buying unused denim with zero signs of wear—a style currently eschewed by the revitalization of vintage-styled menswear where there is great appreciation for the wear of a garment to develop naturally rather than being simulated by the manufacturer. Additionally wearers seek the honor of breaking in every detail of the whiskers at the hip, the color changes at the seat and knee, and frayed hems at the ankle. They buy into the craftsmanship of a well-made item and want to show their experiences while wearing something for a long time. It emphasizes vintage-styled attire that they plan to wear in themselves, and they say they are buying into a mentality and craftsmanship.

Overall, whether it is a punk wearing deconstructed clothes worn in from years of dancing at shows, or an art professor wearing an unusual Kawakubo black dress, or someone in the mainstream wearing jeans ripped up just perfectly along with symbols of convention such as UGG boots and a DKNY oversized sweater, or a fashionable young ad executive breaking in his designer denim, it is all a reflection of the weight of punk's emphasis on commitment to ideals and a DIY viewpoint.

Budget does factor into dress up or down, but it is not only about the ability to buy more items; dress up may be done through creativity more so than cash, and dress down may actually be designer denim and flannel. This can reflect actual financial limitation, or a budget by choice due to feelings of suitable ways to spend money, since there is a large middle- and even upper-class economic ability within the punk community, yet frequently a lower-budget mentality about perceived need and consumerism. This is another aspect of possible conflict, as finances are sometimes spent in mass acquisition of items such as records or books and zines, where the music and text has a higher social value of representing ideas than the artistic manifestation of social ideas presented through the form of a garment. Men's fashion aficionados will spend more for the ideal Levis they plan to own for twenty years. Similarly, independently minded consumers such as punks are willing to pay more when the ideals are intact regarding punk, such as workers' rights, handcrafted goods, limited-run products, and durability.

Rhodes elaborated on the notions of dress up and down regarding some of the influences on her early 1970s designs, noting the Elizabethan slashed silks, Native American beaded pins used as closures and decoration, and holes in a garment that function aesthetically as a printed shape would. All of these she was doing in her high fashions prior to them being adopted in similar forms as punk style. She also placed the development of the punk aesthetics as part of the overall fashion cycle; the soft hippie look would logically be followed by a hard punk look. Satins would turn to leather; brown to black. Thus subculture is not immune to fashion cycles, and does not live completely outside of these motivations. However, with subculture, as discussed, there are numerous motivations driving the dress behaviors, with the fashion cycles playing one role (Interview with author, 2009).

The black leather, metal studs, tight streamlined pants, and the like were a logical progression visually after the hippie culture that was the most prominent subculture predating punk. Also, the aggressive attitude represented symbolically through some of the punk style aesthetic leanings were also cyclical next steps after softer movements right before it (Nika 2011; Polhemus 1994; Zandra Rhodes, Interview with author, 2009). Of course there are bridges with subtle transitions that linked hippie to punk, such as glam and pub rock. Fashion cycles having logical progressions would also be seen in the contrast between laid-back grunge and Riot Grrrl styles of the 1990s, which followed the polished power suit and yuppies of the 1980s.

When Sui or Jacobs have designed punk-inspired clothes they have presented them as natural next waves of fashion design cycles such as the shifting to the Main Street gritty influence of the 1990s away from the Wall Street power dressing of the 1980s. Punks debate this and similar circumstances routinely whenever this happens, as there is a feeling that punk style does exist in the cycle, but also has meanings that extend beyond trend and that the misuse of their appearances has negative ramifications as misrepresentation.

Positive Aspects of Punk Style's Impact

Punk style's widespread growth through mass culture can be perceived as positive. It has effected society's acceptance through mainstreaming of body modifications and the rejection of conventional body type standards, helping develop styles such as geek chic ("nerdcore"[3] as it has been called). These things eventually were adopted in mainstream and high fashion, and thus through the public consciousness as the ideas spread culturally and through fashion.

Globalization has been a significant factor in this growth. Through the Internet, increase in international travel, and relative ease of international shipping of goods,

Fig. 4.9 Contemporary Japanese punk style (copyright Getty, photographer Kaz Chiba, collection Taxi Japan).

the average person has more knowledge and greater accessibility to wider swaths of information on subcultures and related wares. Influences and ideas are rapidly traded back and forth.

Negative Aspects of Punk Style's Impact

This widespread growth can also be perceived as negative. Some punks argue that not everything should be diffused as it is impossible to enact great care through the entire diffusion process, and important ideas are lost in translation from one part of the cycle to the next. This is a universal discussion repeated in many forms whenever a culture's insular styles are reappropriated for public use. Because of conflicts with meaning challenges arise within the originators of these looks as to their take on producing with widespread intent on distribution. There is inner turmoil among those who manage the Ramones' legacy over what is appropriate to merchandise and how, as the products have diversified into all forms of clothing, household goods, and novelty items (Browne 2008). Similarly, those who run Manic Panic decided against going public and becoming full partners with a Japanese company that distributes their goods, citing their contention with bringing outside partners into their inner sanctum, as well as the notion that a corporate partner could change their punk methods (Adams 2007). It is not always the inherent capitalism that troubles the punks, or any group in this quandary, as that is de rigueur, but there is disdain for the misuse of cultural iconography in ways that do not represent their ideals.

These dress products are wildly successful although somewhat controversial for their possible disjuncture from their original meaning as it is crucial to look at the object itself and its use and interpretation (Attfield 2000). Additionally, if an intense object-subject relationship (Attfield 2000) means the myth and object cannot be separated, it makes sense that punks would be frustrated at seeing their iconography displayed at the Mall of America, being sold as a trend instead of a lifestyle. There is the feeling that the outer and most external or accessible parts of punk are being pilfered, without digging to the core meanings. But the question remains whether objects can truly be stripped of their meaning or if individuals can unknowingly represent ideas they may not even understand. It is possible that simultaneously the new mall consumer of these dress items is both presenting a new reinvention of the product and creating a new message, while still representing punk ideas and the former (or remaining) message.

Reinvention of Punk Style

Another important aspect of diffusion is the concept of "reinvention," which Rogers describes as "when adopters change the intended use of an innovation" (2003: 17). It is tied to the manner in which punk style is created to begin with, and is strongly related to reactions to the diffusion process of the style, with the positive and negative aspects that manifest from this process. There are effects on meaning when punk style has been invented and moved through fashion's channels. How mainstream and high fashion reinvent punk styles for their own purposes is a sensitive topic because bricolage and appropriation are how punk dress styles often originate. When punk styles get into nonpunk fashion, there are debates about loss of integrity. But diffusion also influences the fashion and causes reinvention within punk, and many punks want to be part of contemporary styles, but give them a punk spin.

Redoing and remaking items and images to suit new needs is frequently based on some acquired knowledge of the item's meaning and value within visual culture, which Bourdieu (1984) refers to as "cultural capital." It is not mandatory to know the full lineage of an item to work with it, yet for punks that knowledge does provide depth to the selection of items being reinvented as it lends symbolism to the particulars in the way things are retooled (Campbell 2005). Punk consumption and production does require certain cultural capital of the scene's iconography and history, yet it is not elitist in that knowledge is obtainable by most through community involvement in person or, these days, even online.

Each time punk style is created, it uses bricolage and appropriation, and distortion of the original ideas continues as it is shifted away from origins (Hebdige 1979). This is also true of punks who wear previous counterculture styles and have an understanding of the symbol but not necessarily the exact origins. That can exist without hypocrisy as the distorted new look is its own look (Mirzoeff 1998). Some would say that the continued recirculation of the punk images waters down the ideas. But this concept of distortion is precisely what punk dress may have been capturing; that of an inspired copy of their influences and an ironic mirror for those they critiqued. As designs are replicated, mass produced, copied, and changed, it complicates design symbolism and can create multiple layers of meaning (Caplan 2005).

As punk style is widely accepted within all aspects of fashion, there is an increase in the drive within punk to reinvent and express difference. Even with regeneration, though, the classic symbols of punk are revered as the heritage of the movement, regardless of potential loss of potency. The symbols may be accepted as retaining original meaning, even if accepted by a wider audience, and as cues they may still be functional whether blatant or toned down.

Widespread Diffusion Creates Conflict over Meaning

As punk styles are vastly distributed, some of the depth of knowledge regarding the details may be lost in translation. The "know it when I see it" attitude expressed by punks is not without merit, as those tiny signifiers can be quite revealing. Rachel explained, "It has to be put together in a certain way more than it is ... it is hard to describe. I know it when I see it." There is a delicate connection made between people through recognition of small visual cues. Furthermore, for punks concerned with commitment and legitimacy within their culture, this is also how they determine who is an actual insider and who may be a poser. The proper use of cues is very similar to the category of "how it is put together." If the cues are improperly or overly used, they are often seen as an awkward attempt to be cool, and this demonstrates a lack of natural comfort on the part of the wearer. It also may appear the wearer is expressing sentiments that are not fully understood when wearing an array of symbols not commonly worn together by a self-identified punk. However, this judgment, based on perceived limitations of the style—even within the community—leaves little room for the supposedly honored individuality. But it shows a reverence for the time spent by a punk learning cues and teaches punks how to identify one another quickly, including how long they may have been in the community and what subgenres they are interested in. Nate discussed this concept:

> There's so many different genres and subgenres that there really isn't one style. If I see somebody on the street, I can say "OK; this is a punk person versus an indie person or something like that." So I don't think I can give just one answer of what punk fashion is. I think it is such a multifaceted thing. But I know when I see it.

Conclusions

Somewhere in the mix of styles overlapping, the passage of time, and meanings and messages conveyed and transformed, greater overall understanding of one another can emerge. There is potential through punk style to promote a higher appreciation for the various intertwined aspects within our visual and material culture. An example would be that the Ramones have credence as a social and visual symbol with their eye-catching logos and familiar name on T-shirts and merchandise far outpacing record sales (Browne 2008).

Dismantling the myth instilled within the object is complicated with garments that are continually recycled. While much of this attire may have in the past, or may still be loaded with punk meaning, at this time when late twentieth-century styles are at the height of retro popularity, punk imagery may be just vintage imagery enjoyed at the surface level. Current individuals adopting punk styles may not be focused on the punk part, but instead on the trends of a previous decade revived through the fashion cycle.

This does beg the question of why some styles diffuse more effectively than others, and the idea of retro brings this to light. Even if the goal of the modern pre-teen is to dress in a manner inspired by the 1980s, she is in fact frequently donning adaptations of punk styles and not other 1980s phenomena such as shoulder-padded blazers, preppie or yuppie styles, pegged jeans, Michael Jackson leathers, and other trends of that era. Some elements either in the design aesthetics or symbolism have been strong enough in punk styles to be brought to the forefront of current mainstream appeal.

Too much consumption of the past may create an inability or lack of desire to be progressive and think for the future; new innovations and the reenacting of past visions at some point slips past homage and into caricature (Reynolds 2011). Where punk sits in this discussion is complicated. Clark asserted: "the classical subculture 'died' when it became the object of social inspection and nostalgia, and when it became so amenable to commodification" (2003: 224). Overall, through the punk subculture's continued reinvention and diversification, it seems to escape this trap, with the caricature being mostly media hype and not true punk. Clark continued: "The death of subculture has in some ways helped to produce one of the most formidable subcultures yet: the death of subculture is the (re)birth of punk" (225). There is always a past to refer to, a present to critique, and a future to strive for, and the inherent nature of punk is to reinvent through combining these themes. The idea of homage is a form of storytelling and the past does become part of one's own narrative. A different form of homage is when someone is continuing the lineage, building onto the story rather than telling it as a fable (Reynolds 2011). In this way, wearing the styling that existed previously seems very natural on the wearer, as the cues those aesthetics represent are ingrained within them, and they come across not as honoring or critiquing that past, but instead a contemporary continuation of that train of thought, a representation of Brake's (1985) argot. Yet an individual punk may in fact fall into it when adopting an entire punk-style persona of a previous era, rather than including his or her own story into the visual narrative, which was part of the original intensions of punk. However some individuals adopt pieces of histories they admire and place them together atop their selves, rather then embedding those stories into their own narratives.

With punk style, it is generally positive as people are trying to emulate their punk and subcultural ancestors. Some individuals who were among previous generations of punk see this as co-opting their style without living their experience. Yet others feel a bond. Describing punk since the 1970s, Snooky said: "There's a kinship, fashion-wise, between generations and subgenres—to this day we *love* to see kids in mohawks!" This concept can turn cynical, or at least satirical, when irony comes into play. For example, T-shirts are adorned with pop cultural cues shared from another era, such as the childhood of the viewers, and together viewer and wearer get a laugh, share a smile, or wink at their former selves or those who buy into those notions. Thus it is all a form of cultural critique, whether naïve, sincere, robust, ironic, or cynical.

The intended message of punk style is imbued within the creation process, distribution, manner of wearing, and consumption. These aspects of punk style are as pertinent as any particular pattern, color, texture, cut, or fit of a garment. That is why it is a challenge to see looks with punk aesthetics presented with that intent in mind. It is not that there is ownership over the exact aesthetics, as often those were reappropriated themselves, but when stripped of their politics, it is not the same thing. Meaning is not entirely lost on all wearers, however it can be confused, watered down, and personally changed, which viewers will interpret as better, worse, or just new and different, depending on position. As punk style moves through diffusion cycles, there is maintained authenticity and design symbolism that is understood to ongoing generations of self-identified punks, even if the details are known more for the spirit than the specific origin.

Punk dress at shopping malls is a complex display of this postmodern era. It can be seen either as misunderstood and improperly reappropriated symbolic dress, or as a style trend finally blossoming. Either way, punk dress must hold on to some of its design elements to stay iconic, yet must continue to evolve to maintain its relevance. Whether the mass-market consumers realize the significance of the garments they are donning is not the point, as the way they are wearing those looks is creating new messages. Postmodernity would make this hard to swallow at times as a baby born to mainstream parents and an anarcho-punk may be wearing virtually the same sweatshirt. While the reason for using such styles might not be the same, the increased acceptance of variety may be a positive influence of punk on the mainstream. It shows it is not all bad when things get absorbed. It depends on how it is used. Punks use and reappropriate mainstream styles; however when it is reversed there is complication, as the subcultural viewpoint of such items as having stunted creativity, lacking individuality, and a diluted message can feel like an affront to punks. This may be seen as hypocritical by outside observers, but it has a foundation in the critique component of the punk ethos that exists as a more fundamental force behind dress behaviors than the differing forces that drive mainstream dress choices. Punks do purchase things produced for the mainstream but that represent their ideas because of accessibility and affordability, as well as the simple enjoyment and the emotional comfort derived from an item.

Punk style, being so loaded with design symbolism, combined with the reinvention processes, raises the question of whether the garments are in fact part of a traditional diffusion cycle of a trend or whether the similar styles at the Mall of America, Camden Market, or on a table at a basement punk show are actually different things. It could be that punks are innovators and early adopters of a particular aesthetic, and now that look has filtered through the system toward the late adopters and laggards. On the other hand, it could be that punk dress, with its strategic symbolic meaning is similar to that of religious dress or uniforms, which are not actively part of a diffusion cycle, but instead are reappropriated and reinvented in new and possibly meaning-changing ways. This can have the potentially unintended consequence of being controversial among original users (Rogers 2003).

This object-subject relationship (Attfield 2000) is strongly tied to the symbolism the subject feels is within the object and projecting from it. Caplan (2005) said symbolism is a foundation of an object's design. He feels individual consumption is commonly linked to the enjoyment derived from a product, which comes from varied reasons that are often emotional as well as functional. Through this symbolism, people identify with objects, either because of their design specifically, or the way the object was promoted. If the intent is expressing punk meaning through dress, then the specific

Fig. 4.10 Plentiful selection of punk items at Camden Market (copyright Monica Sklar and Harlo Petoskey).

aesthetic details and design could be of less value, as the meaning can be imparted
upon any object once the myth is attached to it. This may be why throughout the forty-
year punk history there have been many types of punk imagery, and new subgenres
keep developing their take on the style. Skaters, emo kids, crusties, and '77 punks each
conceive dress to align with their outlook. However, if the aesthetics and design are
intrinsically linked with the meaning, then it is tough to substitute and reinvent, and
in fact the meanings are lost or corrupted with diffusion. Augie summarized this idea:

> It is the intent behind the item. Because if I wore Fred Perry [brand] knowing that I have
> books and books about mod culture and Oi! [subgenre] culture and I listen to the 4Skins
> [punk/skinhead band], then when I wear that Fred Perry, I'm thinking of something.
> Whereas someone can just walk down the street like in Britain, you get Fred Perrys ev-
> erywhere and all these people aren't punk or Oi!. They never listened to the Oppressed

[band]; don't give a fuck about the 4Skins or Last Resort [bands]. They just think it is a nice tennis shirt. So it is not punk when someone's wearing it who has no conception of its history and how it was co-opted by skins. So it is all in I guess how you brand it yourself. Or you're making a nod to something. Someone else isn't. So one person is punk and one person isn't.

–5–

Summary of Punk Style

Punk is an umbrella concept containing many interrelated variations that share common history and motivations. Self-identified punks describe linking characteristics that construct punk style. Punk is generally rooted in individuals who are in some way disenfranchised from society, by their own choice or being outcast by others. Punk is an ideology that is analytical and critical of the art, politics, popular culture, consumerism, and sexual and social mores of its era.

Punk style is much greater than the collection of aesthetic parts that compose it, both iconic and fleeting. When the visuals are embodied with a punk attitude and themes it is differentiating from its replicas. The way the clothing and body relate and then form a unified new entity is a crucial piece of what composes punk style (Attfield 2000; Brake 1985; DeLong 1998; Eicher 2000). It is much more than placing a ready-made and prescribed garment onto a body and having clear symbolism and purpose as well as a singular meaning. Punk style exists where the person and the form become intertwined. It has transformed many times over, using bricolage and appropriation, to accommodate the counterculture milieu of each era and has also maintained certain signifiers linking it back to core ideas and stylistic concepts. Also, this subculture is flexible and continues to grow and reshape itself to suit the times. Globalization and the Internet influence the choices that go into developing a contemporary style. Influences come from farther reaches, and simultaneously origin stories of a style are lost and found on the Web. This continues the lineage of punk being both a shape shifter and a stalwart. Global cultural expansion has also affected how these styles are produced and consumed. Punk style is now widely available through mainstream channels in addition to the previous manner of being solely constructed by each wearer, or purchased through fanzines (updated to blogs and Etsy online), music and social gatherings, and at independent boutiques.

This, in short, is the most significant change affecting punk style today—the ease with which one can now learn about and obtain a piece of subculture history. With the click of a mouse, and through a few online credit card imprints, one can purchase everything needed to show a fondness for even the most obscure of punk references. Yet this does not mean the interest in those references is sincere and lasting, as easy access enables a fleeting commitment. Questions exist about whether a band T-shirt is inherently more authentically "punk" if its owner purchased it and wore it at a sweaty basement show or from a quick trip to the mall? Same shirt design, different contexts, different levels of punk? Perhaps. But who gets to decide and how does the symbolism of the shirt change per wearer and context?

Traditionally, punk has been built on shared experiences and a long-term commitment to the ideologies that shape the overarching community and the specific subgenres. There are perceptions and then judgments based on how a punk views others' integrity as related to both parties' experiences and ideology, all of which can certainly happen online and perhaps even with greater variety through watching YouTube videos of international acts and chatting on Facebook with punks many time zones away. Thus opportunities to engage in some level of punk experience have not diminished, but the Internet has made it easier to gain exposure to and knowledge of punk. Therefore punks have to decide if challenge, knowledge, or something else altogether is the most pertinent characteristic of punk style.

Subculture, unlike mainstream or high fashion, does not have a governing body—journalists, department store buyers, and color companies—dictating norms and manipulating product availability. But who decides the next wave of punk style and rubber stamps its legitimacy? At what point has it splintered so dramatically it is no longer under the punk umbrella? When is a mohawk one person's service to punk's lineage and another person's trendy costume? This is where argot (Brake 1985) is of great value. Almost all of the punks interviewed for this research discussed a deep-seated desire for emotional comfort, superseding physical comfort, and most indicated satisfying this emotional need required expressing punk ideology through daily actions, such as how they maintain their household, raise their children, what type of job they have, *and* how they dress. This is because for many, their punk identity is salient.

Iconic Punk Styles

Original punk looks were solidified in the eyes of outsiders and the media, and became cues for insiders and for following generations. However, the look is not as much of a uniform as observers would come to stereotype. While punk style has simultaneously maintained some of its original subcultural intent, it has also developed mass appeal, perhaps in an adulterated or appropriated form. This mass image then cyclically helps solidify the stereotypical vision of punk style including such images as lean individuals in tartan plaids, mohawks, distressed black T-shirts, and chunky boots. This has remained a staple of popular culture, yet the styles in use by all who identify as punk constitute a far broader vision that maintains some of those elements and adds new ones. What comprises punk dress is actually a fairly flexible concept with deep roots in cultural motivations that manifest themselves in physical forms, but those forms are not mandated. Contemporary punk dress is drawn from punk origins but also contains influences from other subcultures including mod, goth, hip-hop, and rockabilly. Crafting, high fashion, social and art movements, mainstream trends, and personal interests and daily needs also continually influence it. Additionally, the meanings derived from those iconic pieces have kept some relevance and have also been transformed through time and personalization. Cultural and personal motivations related to an anti-hegemonic attitude, time commitment, and differentiation from others inspire punks to individualize their personal style.

The variation within punk style is motivated by perceptions, identity expression, and cultural influences. A reinvention process keeps the look fresh and expands what is accepted under the punk moniker. It is progressive, yet retains a heritage. Much of punk dress today is heavily coded and subtle, while still harkening back to the iconic pieces of its history. Contemporary punk has many elements that are quite casual and therefore dressed down. However, the heavily stylized elements of the iconic look are present in the level of polish and/or embellishment that exists in almost all

Fig. 5.1 Fashionable style mixing dress up and dress down and paying homage to previous subcultures, UK, 2006 (copyright PYMCA, photographer Liat Chen).

subgenres. Someone who does not appear punk to an observer may be more committed to punk than an outsider may realize, as subtle punk cues are encoded in all sorts of dress. Therefore, punk dress may be more malleable than may be hypothesized. A punk's day-to-day life often reflects a leaning toward subtle and selective cues instead of a full wardrobe of obviously punk fashions. This is based on necessity, age, not wanting to look forced or as if they lack commitment (poser, new), and the influence of other subculture and punk styles such as hardcore and mod that are not as visually different from the mainstream as the 1970s British punk stereotype. Historic influence is highly relevant, and punks are referential to history in their dress, but it is utilized as codes and cues and often not stuck in time donning a stereotypical costume.

Contemporary punk-style garments include jeans, T-shirts, hooded sweatshirts, and athletic shoes, to name a few. This look is about comfort and utilitarianism, not necessarily about avant-garde experimentation or shocking confrontation. It also presents an image of effortless cool with less time spent on presentation, although in contrast there is great pride taken in highly in-the-know details on T-shirts and one-inch buttons, such as obscure band logos. Therefore this does not mean the contemporary leaning toward a casual appearance is "less punk" than one adorned in the iconic styling, as knowing about the cues can take as much time or more than lacing up a pair of classically punk Dr. Martens 1460 boots.

Homage, Cues, and Context as Part of Identity Building

Contemporary punk style is rooted in each scene's aesthetics yet still references the stereotypical form derived from 1970s British styles. Punks are often detail oriented in styling, and understand the relationship of singular components within the whole presentation (DeLong 1998). Elements of design include line, cut and color, and design symbolism as ways to demonstrate cues of wearers' knowledge of punk dress, without showing it in an all-inclusive manner or in a way blatantly obvious to a viewer outsider of the punk subculture. An individual's punk identity expression interweaves cues from historic styles and personal aesthetic preferences.

Through these details of form, punks can develop cues to communicate identity. A selection of punk cues includes a dark color palette with occasional neons; specific patterns such as plaid, stripes, and leopard; oppositional proportions such as narrow bottoms (jeans or hosiery) with large boots; and body modifications and accessories such as tattoos, piercings, cosmetics, and silver jewelry. The use of unnatural hair color is another pertinent part of punk dress, used as a cue to embrace a subversive differentiation from the norm, as well as a nod to the subculture's past.

Cues such as band logos with no text or an all black and silver color palette may be codes meant for insider viewers only or exclusively for self-expression and personal comfort. Therefore, garments and accessories can often be repurposed per context when they can contain multiple cues such as punk subgenre affiliation and workplace appropriateness simultaneously. An example would be a man donning a button-down shirt, blazer, and skinny neck tie in the office, meeting those norms, then heading to the night club, stepping on stage and strapping a guitar on, looking similar to some of the punks that came before him. The textile proportion of his pants may be the only difference, as he may switch from loose-fit khakis to black skinny jeans, therefore changing the overall effect of the look.

This utilization of subcultural style is motivated in a desire to draw attention to the notion of kinship among like-minded people in all that is counterculture, provide visual cues regarding ideals and preferences, and/or promote distinction. Maynard (2004) stressed that people are increasingly self-aware about their visual cues and they dress with strategy and purpose. They want to expend less effort and money, and thus the ideals are woven into the appearance of otherwise conventional clothing. There is a goal to influence culture but also to be insular and oriented toward secret symbolic cues learned through commitment. The core dress items such as shirts, pants, shoes, and haircut may stay the same, however piercings may be removed or displayed, hair may be styled differently, tattoos may be revealed or concealed, and jewelry and hosiery may be changed, all to slant the ensemble toward traditional punk or mainstream styles.

A great deal of what composes punk style is in the wearer's juxtaposition of garments and accessories put together for aesthetic preferences and sociocultural cues, and then embodied in a certain manner in particular contexts. Some punks latch onto their influences and follow the visuals very specifically, but many incorporate strong cues from a preferred subgenre they identify with. They then personalize it and incorporate unique details, with this adaptation accepted as part of the original punk ethos. This can be seen in many aspects of punk styling, such as the choice of fabric patterns.

A primary concern is expressing punk identity in every context, at least to some degree. For punks, dress is primarily motivated by sentiment, with trends in fashion and uses of function secondary, yet not unimportant. The fact punk dress is motivated by ideology and identity expression, yet flexible in form, leads to the clothing fluctuating between crucial or nearly irrelevant to the wearer, as he or she may find other ways to output those intensions such as through decisions regarding career or lifestyle. Thus, multiple identities, particularly those that layer on through aging, are expressed through dress and actions and can survive simultaneously, such as wearing clothing appropriate for work, and those work tasks and attire also representing interests in punk. For some, dressing punk is their strongest expression of that identity. This is especially true of younger individuals.

A punk's experience with subcultural style has a relationship to her clothing choices in nonpunk environments, and yet this is not fully reciprocal. Punks will place punk cues in their nonpunk dress, but not necessarily place nonpunk cues in

Fig. 5.2 Postmodern punk style featuring many influences and personalizations, UK, 2006 (copyright PYMCA, photographer Liat Chen).

their punk dress. Punk influences nonpunk more so than vice versa, and referential and expressive characteristics are frequently utilized to project messages of punk identity salience through one's attire. Specific pieces of clothing may be viewed as punk depending on context, as Converse shoes or a Dickies button-down work shirt may appear standard fare when at the grocery store but have branding and subculture history cues when in punk contexts.

Context factors heavily in punk style choices and interpretations, and how that functions to develop social meanings with ramifications. Punks do dress contextually for situations that can be broken into categories such as work, punk, everyday, and other environments. There are also physical contexts such as age, gender, and the mainstream. A punk individual has a keen awareness of context and makes dress choices in part to suit perceived contextual needs. Punks want to maximize the potential of any environment, whether for physical or emotional comfort, kinship, or communicating a message, which is similar to the goals of almost anyone, punk or not. A salient punk identity can be promoted or toned down depending on how the punk wants to be viewed in any situation and his or her level of confidence per context. This creative use of cues carefully executes transmitting a message to create relationship connections and to position oneself within surroundings. Punks can identify each other by cues, and cues also distinguish punks from mainstream in the nonpunk environment.

Levels of Commitment

Levels of commitment factor into punk dress as deep or lasting efforts provide a rich understanding of visual cues, which can be made use of in overt or subtle manners to aesthetically express punk in any context. On the contrary, the more dedicated one is to other aspects of life, such as occupation, the more willing one is to dress in a manner conventional for that environment. Furthermore, if one's nonpunk context, such as workplace or family life, incorporates punk ideals, one is more willing to dress in the traditional dress of that context rather than overt punk attire, as punk ideals are being expressed through tasks and expressing punk ideals through dress becomes less important. This can be seen in a lawyer willing to don suit and tie when he feels representing the underserved is enacting his punk ideals, or a parent dressing functionally for the playground and feeling confident the way he is raising his children represents his punk ideals.

Internationally there are varied outlooks on linking visual appearance to level of commitment and authenticity. For some cultures, such as in England or Japan, the more time one puts into perfecting visual representation, such as the images related to an in-the-know subculture like punk, the more knowledgeable and committed to the cause they are seen to be. In the United States, there tends to be a goal for an effortless appearance, and thus a naturalistic emphasis, even if feigned, can reign. Items that are well-worn, distressed, or old demonstrate a lived-through experience and express dedication. This is where some of the conflict develops about buying reissued items such as reprinted T-shirts at Hot Topic.

A willingness to spend a great deal of money or seek out specialty items is another signifier of allegiance, such as having limited-edition pieces, items made by hand, and original issues. Sometimes the cost for these garments is highly elevated, which itself is a sign of devotion to some if paying that cost is generally prohibitive but someone is willing to do it who is not otherwise wealthy. The expense of clothing drives most punks not to want items that are disposable, which reflects a lack of earthly compassion, financial responsibility, and commitment to the identity components of the aesthetics of dress.

Motivations for Wearing Punk Dress

The style today shows respect for previous subcultures by using historic styles as a guidebook although not as a rulebook. Punk form is tied to cultural and physical motivations. These cultural and physical factors inform how punks use dress, but these factors do not dictate strict parameters for form. Context often plays a role in how the motivations are acted out through dress behaviors and how an individual feels the style will control the resulting social interactions. Punks do want to stay somewhat current with trends, even in the broadest form, or within demographic norms such as "dressing one's age," which is a matter of perspective to some degree. They do not always look as different from the mainstream as an outsider would think, and instead it is often about the detailed cues and insider knowledge they like to use to express themselves and to distinguish real from poser punks.

All of this takes into consideration the longevity of punk as an ideology that can sustain an individual's life cycle, but needs to be adjusted based on aging and life cycles that bring financial concerns, bodily changes, family growth, and occupational responsibilities. Over time this frequently results in a wardrobe that expresses a salient punk identity yet can function in multiple situations.

A Group Experience and an Individual Experience

Dressing in punk style is simultaneously a collective and an individual experience (Bloustien 2003). Community symbols combined with personalization are key to making punk style one's own. Individualization is mixed with subtle ties to genre uniforms. Groups are of value as they inform the ideas of the cultural and motivational factors as well as the splinters and subgenres that direct forms. There is a strong motivation to use cues through dress to identify with a group and align with those ideas and participants in the culture. Naturally, most people want to make friends and feel understood. However these are also individuals with personal life needs and preferences. Therefore some wear subcultural uniforms of sorts, while others wear nothing identifiable as subcultural yet they still consider themselves punk. Most fall somewhere in between.

The perspective is relevant, whether it is the viewer as self (personal expression) or in conjunction with viewer as third party, and only mildly has to do with dressing for social expectations. Punks do dress to meet the subculture norms of their community, but also feel dress freedom within those parameters and are mostly concerned with pleasing themselves. The greatest concern tends to be a potential loss of a punk cultural identity and expressing a personal identity, much more so than on properly styling particular visual signifiers. This mildly conflicts with the notion of the detail-oriented punk who other punks can read through cues, yet it does allow room for individuality as well as support the idea that once one has built so much

Fig. 5.3   Punk style that demonstrates group and individual representations, as well as blatant and subtle cues (copyright Getty, photographer and credit Fotosearch Premium).

cultural capital he can express aspects of it without cashing in on the whole lot at
any one time.

Postmodernism and Globalization as Influences on Contemporary Dress

Almost any object for dress can be deemed punk. Some artifacts may not be a part
of the original iconic stereotype, but are made into the punk likeness by the wearer.
If the intent is expressing punk concepts through the vehicle of dress, then the specific aesthetic details and design could be of little value, as the meaning can be attached to any object aligned with the ideology. Consequently, the variety of opinions
on what composes punk dress reflects this postmodern attitude. Also, ideas about

differentiation and personalization as important within punk ideals indicate the value of nonuniform thought.

Previous subcultures and current cultural influences merge together, combined with the diversity of the background of the people who make up the punk community. When contextual dressing is added into the mix, a blend of postmodern hodgepodge is accepted as punk style. Punk was never a centralized movement, yet it always rotated around core groups and ideas. Postmodernity would see punk morph and splinter with a variety of styles acceptable under the umbrella concept that is punk. Many take the punk spirit and pick and choose visual signifiers to latch on to, making punk in conjunction with the values of this era.

Furthermore, postmodernism permits individuality in interpretations of punk style as wearer and viewer, which is how it can retain relevance for a self-identified punk and for someone who buys garments reflecting it as a trend in the mainstream. Postmodernism is also a way individuals embrace ideas from various aspects of life and employ multiple concepts simultaneously, all with their own body of knowledge informing decisions (Efland, Freeman, and Stuhr 1996; Henderson and De-Long 2000; Sturken and Cartwright 2001). Each generation further expands punk ideas and the resulting dress, and then the mainstream continues to appropriate those styles. Through divergent levels of personal commitment, varied time periods when one discovered and embraced punk, and diverse individual experiences, the opinions about punk dress within punk circles can widely vary.

Is Punk Style Still Extreme?

In the 1970s, punk style was an affront to conventional society. Roger said: "Middle England was shocked and horrified. I remember going to Paris wearing a God Save The Queen T-shirt with a pin through it, and people were just...[it was] really quite threatening. Older generation people would come up to me, my wife and I, 'How dare you deface the queen,' and that's another country...I think also that really, the whole punk thing was really the last major fashion that really kind of happened in a way because after that it was all derivatives of in one way or another" (Interview with author, 2009). A debate rages over how edgy it remains now that the style has so vastly diversified and been adopted by high fashion and mainstream repeatedly.

The look is still testing boundaries and shocking viewers, yet with an increased level of complexity from its initial incarnations. The idea that contemporary punks continue to find satisfaction in dressing with punk cues, as well as encounter a need to consider accommodations when not in punk contexts validates its effectiveness. Punks perceive the need to cover their tattoos, take out their facial piercings, and wear less blatant punk cues when in nonpunk contexts. They conceive whole systems of accommodations, which cyclically reinforces the power of the norm they are complying with and the potency of the visual they are tempering. It goes to the

Fig. 5.4 God Save The Queen T-shirt, original shirt produced using DIY method, designed by Westwood and McLaren. This is a copy made for the 1986 film *Sid & Nancy* by some of the same people involved with the original design (copyright the Contemporary Wardrobe Collection, photograph Roger K. Burton).

more drastic examples such as interviewee Ben losing his job for appearing in a form of punk dress (the nude) even though he did not dress that way at his work. Unnatural hair colors and unconventional haircuts have become increasingly acceptable in some mainstream contexts, yet remain a point of contention in other situations. However, while this is often true in casual affairs and the entertainment industry, it often is not acceptable with the formalities of a conventional workplace; thus, there is still a subversive quality to green, pink, and blue hair.

Numerous stories from current headlines prove punk style remains controversial. Acceptance of its growth toward the mainstream, and as a trend at times, is not universal. Variations on punk style play a direct role in the persecution of some wearers. The wearer may not even self-identify as punk, and be aligned with its history and ideology, yet the style is so imbued with meaning that cannot be fully stripped through any diffusion process that it continues to have relevance in numerous contexts.

"The first phase of punk styling, between 1976 and 1977 was most probably the last time in social history that clothing would provoke such hatred" (Stolper and Wilson 2004: 10). While that original distaste may have lost some of its gusto in Western society, it does retain an impact. A wearer of punk style may want those styles incorporated for full acceptance of diverse standards of attractiveness, and yet the same wearer also probably dons the attire for its potent antiauthority components. In the United States, students who dye their hair in colors deemed unsuitable or who wear mohawks to school have been disciplined. The school administrations' reasons center around the supposed distracting nature of unconventional hair that detours students from focusing on their studies. The students' challenge of the rules falls in line with punk originators' ideals, as notions of beauty standards are debated. Disciplined students address the fact that peers with hair dyed in what are perceived as natural colors, albeit not natural to that individual, are not subject to criticism ("Student Kicked Out of School" 2008; "School Officials Tell" 2008).

In non-Western cultures, punk style is still fresh and sometimes moving through that culture's awareness for the first time. Examples include the stoning, torture, and killing of youth dubbed emos in Iraq, where the subculture is perceived as having homosexual overtones—primarily in appearance—which is treated as a negative ("Emos in Iraq Being Killed at Alarming Rate" 2012). Additionally, in Indonesia, individuals adorned in punk style at a punk band's music event were rounded up and jailed, then forced to bathe, cut their hair, change their clothes, and pray ("Indonesian Punks Detained" 2011). These international incidents at all levels of severity reinforce the value in the design.

Punk Identity Salience and Negotiation of Appearances

The ongoing shock value from punk style presents a challenge for punks who face decisions about multiple salient identities, such as job roles, social obligations, and religious leanings. Balancing different identities is a challenge for anyone, and for a punk it can be especially significant as it can be the opposing pull of necessity and ideology. For many, punk is not a hobby akin to gardening or playing piano, but a lifestyle that needs to be reflected in some manner through that individual's actions. Whether through dress or tasks, the salient identity needs to show itself.

For the interviewees appearance labor was linked to emotional comfort, pushing boundaries, having jobs that incorporate punk ideals, and using phrases including "needing to feel like me." Snooky added: "Punk style still resonates today because people love the spirit of rebellion, and the DIY attitude. It's still relevant...There may be less shock value, but it's still artistically/individually expressive" (Interview with author, 2012). A punk identity is deemed equally or more important than nonpunk identities, and conflict arises because punks can see the value in embracing each of those nonpunk identities as well, be it for the workplace, parenthood, religion, hobby, or other facet of life. The way they consider their punk and nonpunk identities is not one-dimensional, but nuanced; this is reflected in their dress behaviors. Perspectives on dress are adjusted as a punk increases time spent in each context, moves upward within the environment, experiences demographic changes such as age and geography, and feels a strong sense of commitment, acceptance, and positive standing in context.

Punks do find ways to make their style perform for them. This subculture's relationship to postmodernity can contribute to accommodating for appearance labor because the lack of a prescribed uniform for punk means there can be more flexibility while staying in touch with one's salient punk identity. Also, much of dressing for punk is about viewer as self (personal expression) in conjunction with viewer as third party, and takes into consideration dressing for social expectations then decides how to function within or outside of the perceived boundaries of a context.

Emotional comfort based on how one uses aesthetics to express an identity is important to the wearer and makes him or her feel good. This goes hand in hand with people being able to accept or at least properly understand punk dress; thus it can be worn in a worthwhile manner because it is understood. That understanding does not have to result in acceptance or approval; it can be meaningfully confrontational, that is, it can evoke discourse beyond shock value with some amount of intent on the wearer's part, even if that intent is about self-expression and results in a dialogue from someone who has viewed and wants to discuss their way of representing themselves through the bold slogans on T-shirts and those types of appearance. An understanding nonetheless leads to emotional comfort because one is expressing oneself and being heard (through being seen). It is validating to the wearer to feel he or she can express himself or herself accurately in this world, and part of that is not only being able to find the stylistic tools to put ideas out there, but also how those ideas will be interpreted.

There is benefit in aesthetically expressing internal feelings. The punk interviewees use words such as "happy" and "comfortable" regarding their emotional state when they feel they succeed in this process. This feeling of being content as a result of the dress choices they have made for their identity expression indicates experiencing low or reduced appearance labor. Punks have the greatest success (and possibly the least appearance labor) when they find a way to express their punk identity within the perceived limitations of appropriate dress. However, punks are rarely willing to get this comfort at all costs.

Emotional comfort is a goal to strive for although it is often met with challenges of expression and viewer (mis)interpretation. Since punk style is about expressing an identity and ideology, when it is characterized through images of singular garments or "looks" it can be perceived as naïve and even interpreted negatively according to punks. There is often disdain and disappointment when groups are reduced to fashion descriptions as a signifier for the entirety of who they are. This has continued to be seen in the use of the iconic punk image as a media stereotype, and has been throughout the subgenres as well, such as in the 1990s when the Riot Grrrls were often described in mainstream magazines not by their actions, their music, or their texts, but solely by their dress (Marcus 2010).

Many punks scoff at the media version of themselves presented in reductionary terms, feeling they are characterized too narrowly rather than through a robust discussion of the many facets of their lives and ideologies. This is a legitimate complaint when observers deem certain garments as representative of societies, even when separated from body and soul, let alone from context. However, within punk, the concept of fashion is confused, as it does not equal bad, since it is a form of identity and artistic expression; yet the word itself, and for some, spending too much time on it, indicates a lack of sincerity and a misguided focus. Therefore, fashion is often seen as a slur or a passing trend. Thus when punks are assessed based on appearances, they may become reactionary as there is the idea it is not the complete picture and lacks an understanding of all of the motivations interlaced throughout the visuals.

The motivations and the apparel body construct (DeLong 1998) hold more weight than the form of any particular garment, therefore legitimizing the venomous reaction from punks being evaluated as parts instead of as the sum. Punk style is embodied and when viewed by an outsider, a third party, a conflict may perpetually remain, as proper representations are always subject to interpretation, especially when there is fluidity of options for these nonprescribed forms. The garments themselves are only a part of the argot. However there is some potential for punks to be overly reactionary and completely shrug off all iconographic representations and media, which address the physicality, as the form is a valuable facet of a punk identity. Furthermore, for youth, it is sometimes the *most* empowering tool for expression, prior to career employment, financial, and family choices made when one is in adulthood, that can express a punk ideology through other actions. There remains an ongoing conflict within punk to want to use its symbols for expression, and to be understood by them and affiliated with their meanings, yet conversely to be angered when a viewer does take those symbols to construct meanings about the individual. Using the expressive and referential characteristics that purposefully position one as antiauthoritarian and/or counter the main culture, in critique of it, does invite a discussion of that positing. However, using tattoos, thick-soled boots, or dark colors to position oneself as outside of mainstream groupthink does not then mean the arena one has chosen to reside within contains lesser moral or educational standards, for example. This is where the conflict takes its more convoluted shape. Someone might want to be seen as antimainstream society, but they do want to acknowledge that the alternate society they have built contains quality people.

Where Can Punk Style Continue to Go?

Punk style will remain part of the aesthetic of young people expressing distinction, of adults who embrace alternative appearances and lifestyles, and of high fashion and mainstream fashion indefinitely. Splinter subgenres will continue to branch, but will also continue to revere the past and keep those aspects that remain incendiary with the mainstream. The postmodern value placed on many methods, solidified through the Internet and continued globalism, will promote this continued splintering. It also does draw some back to a root form, trying to find common threads and trace history. This is correspondent to suit and ties or religious garb that maintains social worth; any style built around an ideology tends to have more resonance than one built around stylistic trends of an era. It will continue to be adjusted by time, circumstance, and prominent members of the subculture, as well as adapted by individuals to suit their own needs. Yet the basic tenets of the style will remain and will maintain similar meanings. In the end, the general components that punk rallies against have permanent places within culture, and punk is one manner to deal with them.

The mainstream will continue to incorporate aspects of punk style. This trendiness will bring in new audiences to punk, bring fresh punk designs to enliven conventional styles, and drive subcultural reinvention to maintain distinction (Clark 2003). It also will continue to make punk accessible in a manner that makes it more feasible for people to embrace and have mainstream lives, for better or worse regarding punk's ideals. Merchandising of punk will escalate, but merchandising within punk will grow more sophisticated and will spread its wings, making for more success of varied members. There may be even less centralization than before, when people would gather their ideas around bands, stores, record labels, zine writers, and political activists, as the numbers of each of those will grow and the contribution of any one may be less measurable. But their outreach has expanded, and this give and take will certainly impact punk style.

The stylistic details may need to keep changing and growing through time, because of postmodernism and globalization, to keep their relevance as cultural shifts, such as those toward more acceptance of nontraditional lifestyles and mass adoption, subtly effect the overall style. What may get lost along the way is some of the knowledge of what the original reference was about and how the bricolage got established. Just as many do not know the origin of why neckties are worn with business suits, the contemporary cultural significance of that necktie is not diminished in the boardroom. This may be true of blue mohawks or Dr. Martens boots.

Because of the collective fuzzy memory of how garments originated, yesterday's shocking items may be tomorrow's norm and new controversial images may need to emerge to maintain punk's position as edgy. Punk style, however, is not only confrontational for argument's sake, but also to expand minds regarding acceptance or others' appearances. So when a punk style does in fact becomes more commonplace, it devalues that particular garment's shock value, but applauds that item's journey

Fig. 5.5 Contemporary young woman evoking a punk aesthetic (copyright Veer, photograph Kuzma).

into increasing tolerance by the mainstream. This is part of the need for punk style to reinvent. By maintaining distinctiveness from mainstream society and carving out a space for linking like-minded others, each time a punk style gets accepted it can be viewed as an accomplishment. This fact is sometimes lost in discussions of the mainstreaming of punk style. As Snooky argued: "As long as there are rebels, non-conformists, and creative people, punk style will always be a part of fashion" (Interview with author, 2012).

One lasting result of punk may be that since its inception few other subcultures have usurped its continued relevance and ongoing relationship to fashion. "Punk changed the world—arguably more so than any other single style tribe before or since" (Polhemus 1994: 93). Hip-hop has traveled the most similar path. People always want to look for the next big fashion thing that will change the way humanity evaluates itself and individuals express their inner selves. Hippies were counterculture, but faded and now their style is nostalgic in many ways. Punk has been willing to reinvent and include other variants; therefore it stays relevant, and can go on indefinitely in some capacity. This is especially true as the object-subject relationship (Attfield 2000) and the apparel body construct (DeLong 1998) crucial to the authenticity of punk allow for a key component, the persons themselves, and therefore it is all about the relationship of wearers to clothes, contexts, and interpretations. This gives equal value in the equation to the form and the wearer, and, as each one changes and grows, the other can balance it to stay aligned with punk.

Closing

Through my own aging process I am learning how to maintain aspects of a punk appearance while finding my new aspects of life are quite salient as well, and require visual attention and expression. Also, the hodge-podge included in punk style is becoming quite varied. There are so many tools to draw on for daily dressing that, when I tie it all together, sometimes it doesn't read as punk as I feel I am. I am relatively okay with this, although it does lead to pause for thought at times. I recently posted my photo on a punk site and someone said, "Oh, you do not look so punk; good to see it's still on the inside," yet in other contexts I certainly don't look like the norm. Physical and cultural contexts, such as my demographics, play a role in how the style continues to evolve in my life.

Another way I see the future of punk is through my child's eyes. He will find it all new again and develop fresh insights on the boundaries of culture and how to live within and outside of them. I will try to impart the ideologies I hold dear, including some punk perspectives and appreciation for the visual stylistic components. Yet how he finds his way through mass culture and counterculture is yet to be seen, and it is too early to predict what subcultural trends will emerge in his lifetime.

I do know his views on punk style are already starting to be shaped. While in line at a warehouse retailer recently, a person with another small child stood in front of us. Her child was staring at my (at the time) black, pink, red, and orange hair. The little girl said she liked it and asked me if she could do that to her hair. I told her she would need to ask her mom, and her mom chuckled, but quickly turned away—not exactly in disdain or disgust, but as if it was purely funny and not worth consideration. Granted, the girl was quite young, but the mother was already presenting her with an air of mockery at the concept. Then I looked down at my son, and thought about how he does not even know any different than a mom with rainbow hair, piercings, tattoos, or whatever version of punk style I happen to be embracing. Most likely if roles were reversed he would not be driven to stare, nor to ask permission and be scoffed off at something like that. Sure he has visuals that remain unfamiliar to him, and will undoubtedly inquire; however those types of instances remind me about punk's continued relevance, ideas of tolerance, and the progress that has been made. In the end, it was just two moms waiting in line for groceries, both probably with dyed hair, and we were so similar and so different simultaneously. It made me think of our children as the next generation of people who will shape interpretations of punk style, regardless of whether either of those children grow to be subcultural insiders, outsiders, or someone in between.

Notes

Chapter 1: Introduction

1. The Spitz article discusses the documentary film entitled *1991: The Year Punk Broke* directed by Dave Markey. Spitz said,

   > Even the title is something of a joke, first uttered by Mr. Markey, a director in Los Angeles who had flown to London with Nirvana that August. ("Those guys had just been up all night shooting the video for 'Smells Like Teen Spirit,' and I think Kurt had clashed with the director.") As Mr. Markey recovered from jet lag with members of Sonic Youth at a hotel in Ireland, they watched Mötley Crüe on MTV playing a cover of "Anarchy in the U.K." by the Sex Pistols. "And I just said, '1991 is the year punk broke,' " Mr. Markey recalled. "They kind of snickered, and from there we all started saying it to each other. Proudly self marginalizing, the notion of punk ever breaking out seemed absurd."

2. Infamous bassist of the band the Sex Pistols.
3. Often cited "the year punk exploded," such as in a 2007 *Spin Magazine* cover article by Charles Aaron, 1977 is seen as a significant year for punk. The influential band Bad Brains started that year, punks raised a ruckus on the popular Bill Grundy program in London, many influential albums came out, and significant music events took place; therefore it was the point when the media and the masses really picked up on punk and it became a bit of a trend. The iconic punk in the United Kingdom started then from a mass point of view, so saying something or someone is '77 can be an insult or a compliment as it represents both the first wave of trendy types and diehards to an original era.
4. An exception was made in the case of Brian Peterson, who is referred to by full name because there is also an interviewee named Brian.
5. TAMS is computer software used for coding and analysis of qualitative research such as transcribed interviews.
6. Subgenres of punk will be described in later chapters.

Chapter 2: Punk Style Past and Present

1. There is a significant volume of critique and discussion within the museum and fashion editorial communities regarding large-scale exhibitions focused

on fashion designs, fashion designers, and aspects of twentieth- and twenty-first-century popular culture that emphasize the use of dress. The discussion revolves around whether the dress objects are worthy of museum display or whether the exhibitions solely exist to draw crowds based on familiarity, not intellectual analysis.

2. Straight edge is a subgenre of hardcore and a subgenre of punk. It is sometimes referred to as sXe, initially because of the X associated with it that would be written on hands for a person who was underage at a show and would not be drinking. It is a lifestyle movement that started in the early 1980s, and it is named after a song by the influential band Minor Threat that discussed abstaining from sex and drugs. It would become a facet of the hardcore punk and emo movements of the 1980s and 1990s where sociopolitical choices were becoming dominant aspects of the punk community. It would maintain that but also develop controversy surrounding groups that some associated as criminal or delinquent gangs functioning primarily out of Boston and Salt Lake City. The original perspective and the gangs are not specifically overlapping in their participants, motivations, or actions.

3. In the early twentieth century, piercing of any body part in the Western world was uncommon for men or women. However, after World War II, it increased in popularity for gay men and eventually women. Punk picked it up in the 1970s using safety pins and adding places beyond the earlobes. Proponents of modern primitivism introduced international piercing traditions, such as the stretching of the lobes, to Western culture. The leaders of the piercing and the modern primitivism interests produced the first texts on the subject; they also supported the opening of piercing studios.

4. The Bromley Contingent gained this moniker in an article by journalist Caroline Coon, and it was shorthand to describe a well known punk group of individuals based on the suburb where some of them lived.

5. This subgenre frequently wore argyle sweater vests and vintage cardigans.

6. This subgenre was named "math" because of the time signature of the music being complex and unusual; the individuals who practiced it were often bookish as well.

7. This subgenre was named as such primarily based on the dark, straight, brushed-forward, almost Caesar-style haircut that was preferred, and was exacerbated by the sometimes sallow skin that came from adherents often abiding by a vegan diet in an incomplete manner that did not provide them sufficient nutrition.

Chapter 3: Punk Style Motivations and Explanations

1. This was a shop run by those who considered themselves modern primitives, and some shops gained the same level of prestige as acclaimed tattoo parlors.

2. Some bands attract dedicated fans who, when grouped together, often maintain similar aesthetics and lifestyle and have a very unified presence; thus they are called armies.
3. Lead singer of the band Bikini Kill.
4. Independent record label based out of Washington, DC.

Chapter 4: Punk Style and Society

1. There has been much debate over the alleged counterfeits on the market, with McLaren and Westwood not always agreeing on what they actually did make and how much of it. Also their son, as an adult, has owned a fashion businesses remaking things he was involved in making the first time around when he was a youth. Furthermore, brands, designers, boutiques and small manufacturers using images or shapes that were originally punk styles, some with image permission from original designers and some without permission. Some even made it into museum exhibitions, and a large-scale auction was called off as the objects' authenticity (as having originated in the 1970s) was called into question. Westwood won a court case against one mainstream manufacturer who was producing garments that used old branding of her punk lines. There is a further layer of controversy on all of this, as much of punk consists of reappropriated garments, although the intention was to knowingly create a new piece, often with a layer of sarcasm or political comment. But the new intention is to copy and profit from those thinking they were made by those with punk intentions or by people who do not share the punk intentions and are strictly making new garments, such as the Mall of America; where it differs from the Westwood case is they are directly lifting her logos and images, rather than homage styling (Hollington 2008).
2. One such site (and now book) is "lookatthisfuckinghipster.tumblr.com" which is part insider, good-natured self-deprecating humor, and part mockery when a subculture or street style appearance seems trite, pretentious, or insincere.
3. "Core" is a suffix often added to otherwise nonpunk words to frame that idea within a punk context and add a punk perspective. It is a slang offshoot of the word *hardcore*; although the ideas it may be aligned with may not have to do with the subgenre of hardcore itself, the *core* part is the notion of insular community, committed center of thought, and dedication.

References

Aaron, Charles. 2007. "1977: The Year Punk Exploded." *Spin*, September 20. http://www.spin.com/1977/. Accessed September 9, 2012.

Adams, Courtney Lee. 2007. "The Martha Stewart of Punk Rock?" *Business Week*, August 8. http://www.businessweek.com/stories/2007–08–08/the-martha-stewart-of-punk-rock-businessweek-business-news-stock-market-and-financial-advice. Accessed January 17, 2013.

AirWair Limited. 1999. *Dr. Martens*. England: AirWair Limited.

Attfield, Judy. 2000. *Wild Things: The Material Culture of Everyday Life*. Oxford: Berg.

Baron, Stephen. 1989. "Resistance and Its Consequences: The Street Culture of Punks." *Youth & Society* 21(2): 207–37.

Beeber, Steven. 2006. *The Heebie-Jeebies at CBGB's: A Secret History of Jewish Punk*. Chicago: Chicago Review Press.

Bennett, Andy. 1999. "Subcultures or Neo-Tribes? Rethinking the Relationship between Youth, Style and Musical Taste." *Sociology* 33(3): 599–617.

Bennett, Andy. 2006. "Punk's Not Dead: The Continuing Significance of Punk Rock for an Older Generation of Fans." *Sociology* 40(2): 219–35.

Bloustien, David. 2003. "'Oh Bondage, Up Yours!' Or Here's Three Chords, Now Form a Band: Punk, Masochism, Skin, Anaclisis, Defacement." In *The Post-Subcultures Reader*, ed. David Muggleton and Rupert Weinzierl, 51–64. Oxford: Berg.

Blumer, Herbert. 1969. "Fashion: From Class Differentiation to Collective Selection." *Sociological Quarterly* 10: 275–91.

Blush, Steven. 2001. *American Hardcore: A Tribal History*. Los Angeles: Feral House.

Bourdieu, Pierre. 1984. *Distinction: A Social Critique of the Judgment of Taste*. Cambridge, MA: Harvard University Press.

Brake, Mike. 1985. *Comparative Youth Culture: The Sociology of Youth Culture and Youth Subcultures in America, Britain, and Canada*. New York: Routledge.

Browne, David. 2008. "Hey! Ho! Let's Shop!" *Spin*, February, 35–36.

Busch, Akiko. 2001. "Perspectives on Craft and Design." In *Objects for Use: Handmade by Design*, ed. Paul J. Smith, 8–10. New York: Harry N. Abrams.

Calluori, Raymond. 1985. "The Kids Are Alright: New Wave Subcultural Theory." *Social Text* 12: 43–53.

Campbell, Colin. 2005. "The Craft Consumer: Culture, Craft, and Consumption in a Postmodern Society." *Journal of Consumer Culture* 5(1): 23–42.

Caplan, Ralph. 2005. *By Design: Why There Are No Locks on Bathroom Doors in the Hotel Louis XIV and other Object Lessons*. New York: Fairchild.

Cherry, Brigid, and Maria Mellins. 2011. "Negotiating the Punk in Steampunk: Subculture, Fashion and Performative Identity." *Punk and Post Punk* 1(1): 5–25.

Clark, Dylan. 2003. "The Death and Life of Punk the Last Subculture." In *The Post-Subcultures Reader*, ed. David Muggleton and Rupert Weinzierl, 223–36. Oxford: Berg.

DeLong, Marilyn. 1998. *The Way We Look: Dress and Aesthetics*. 2nd ed. New York: Fairchild.

Doy, Gen. 2000. *Black Visual Culture: Modernity and Postmodernity*. New York: St. Martin's Press.

Duffty, Keanan, and Paul Gorman. 2009. *Rebel Rebel: Anti-Style*. New York: Universe.

Efland, Arthur, Kerry Freedman, and Patricia Stuhr. 1996. *Postmodern Art Education: An Approach to Curriculum*. Reston, VA: National Art Education Association.

Eicher, Joanne. 2000. "Dress." In *Routledge International Encyclopedia of Women: Global Women's Issues and Knowledge*, ed. Cheris Kramarae and Dale Spender, 422–3. New York: Routledge.

"Emos in Iraq Being Killed at Alarming Rate." 2012. *New York Daily News*, March 12. http://articles.nydailynews.com/2012–03–12/news/31156220_1_southern -baghdad-neighborhood-cement-blocks-iraq-specialist. Accessed August 29, 2012.

Evans, Caroline. 1997. "Dreams That Only Money Can Buy...Or, The Shy Tribe in Flight from Discourse." *Fashion Theory* 1(2): 169–88.

Faiers, Jonathan. 2008. *Tartan*. Oxford: Berg.

Featherstone, Mike. 1999. "Body Modification: An Introduction." *Body & Society* 5(1): 1–12.

Finley, Susan. 2003. "Arts-Based Inquiry in QI: Seven Years from Crisis to Guerilla Warfare." *Qualitative Inquiry* 9(2): 281–96.

Fiske, John. 1992. "The Cultural Economy of Fandom." In *The Adoring Audience: Fan Culture and Popular Media*, ed. Lisa Lewis, 30–9. Oxford: Routledge.

Fox, Kathryn Joan. 1987. "Real Punks and Pretenders: The Social Organization of a Counterculture." *Journal of Contemporary Ethnography* 16(3): 344–70.

Force, William Ryan. 2009. "Consumption Styles and the Fluid Complexity of Punk Authenticity." *Symbolic Interaction* 32(4): 289–309.

Freitas, Anthony, Susan Kaiser, Joan Chandler, Carol Hall, Jung-Won Kim, and Tania Hammidi. 1997. "Appearance Management as Border Construction: Least Favorite Clothing, Group Distancing, and Identity Not!" *Sociological Inquiry* 67(3): 323–35.

Gilmore, Mikal. 1998. *Night Beat: A Shadow History of Rock & Roll*. New York: Anchor Books.

Gilmore, Mikal. 2011. "The Fury and the Power of The Clash." *Rolling Stone*, March 3, 60–67, 79.

Goffman, Erving. 1959. *The Presentation of Self in Everyday Life*. New York: Anchor Books.

Gorman, Paul. 2010. "Andrew Bunney's Studs-We-Like." *The Look Blog*, February 25. http://rockpopfashion.com/blog/?p = 230. Accessed January 17, 2013.

Gray, Marcus. 2004. *The Clash: Return of the Last Gang in Town*. Milwaukee, WI: Hal Leonard.

Hall, Stuart, and Tony Jefferson. 1976. *Resistance through Rituals: Youth Subcultures in Post War Britain*. London: Routledge.

Hebdige, Dick. 1979. *Subculture: The Meaning of Style*. London: Routledge.

Henderson, Betsy, and Marilyn DeLong. 2000. "Dress in a Postmodern Era: An Analysis of Aesthetic Expression and Motivation." *Clothing and Textiles Research Journal* 18(4): 237–50.

Holland, Samantha. 2004. *Alternative Femininities: Body, Age, and Identity*. Oxford: Berg.

Hollington, Kris. 2008. "Are You Feeling Lucky Punk?" *The Daily Mail*, August 28. http://www.mailonsunday.co.uk/home/moslive/article-1046965/Are -feeling-lucky-punk.html#. Accessed August 21, 2012.

"Indonesian Punks Detained and Shaved by Police." 2011. *The Guardian*, December 14. http://www.guardian.co.uk/world/2011/dec/14/indonesian-punks -detained-shaved-police. Accessed August 29, 2012.

James, William. 1890. *Principles of Psychology*. New York: Holt Rinehart and Winston.

Kawamura, Yuniya. 2005. *Fashion-ology: An Introduction to Fashion Studies*. Oxford: Berg.

Klein, Naomi. 1999. *No Logo: 10th Anniversary Edition*. New York: Picador.

Leblanc, Lauraine. 1999. *Pretty in Punk: Girl's Gender Resistance in a Boy's Subculture*. New Brunswick, NJ: Rutgers University Press.

Levine, Harold, and Steven Stumpf. 1983. "Statements of Fear through Cultural Symbols: Punk Rock as a Reflective Subculture." *Youth and Society* 14(4): 417–35.

Marcus, Griel. 1990. *Lipstick Traces: A Secret History of the Twentieth Century*. Cambridge, MA: Harvard University Press.

Marcus, Sara. 2010. *Girls to the Front: The True Story of the Riot Grrrl Revolution*. New York: Harper Perennial.

Masquelier, Adeline. 2005. *Dirt, Undress, and Difference: Critical Perspectives on the Body's Surface*. Bloomington: Indiana University Press.

Maynard, Margaret. 2004. *Dress and Globalisation*. Manchester: Manchester University Press.

McCracken, Grant. 1988. *Culture and Consumption: New Approaches to the Symbolic Character of Consumer Goods and Activities*. Bloomington: Indiana University Press.

McKenna, Kristine. 1999. "Remembrance of Things Fast." In *Forming: The Early Days of L.A. Punk*, ed. Track 16 Gallery, 26–37. Santa Monica, CA: Smart Art Press.

McNeil, Legs, and Gillian McCain. 1996. *Please Kill Me: The Uncensored Oral History of Punk*. New York: Grove Press.

Mead, George Herbert. 1934. *Mind, Self and Society*. Chicago: University of Chicago Press.

Mirzoeff, Nicholas. 1998. *The Visual Culture Reader*. Oxford: Routledge.

Muggleton, David. 2002. *Inside Subculture: The Postmodern Meaning of Style*. Oxford: Berg.

Mutanen, Ulla-Maaria. 2007. "My Logo, Not No Logo." *Craft* 2: 20.

Nedorostek, Nathan, and Anthony Pappalardo. 2008. *Radio Silence: A Selected Visual History of American Hardcore Music*. New York: MTV Press.

Nicolay, Megan. 2006. *Generation T: 108 Ways to Transform a T-Shirt*. New York: Workman.

Nika, Colleen. 2011. "Anna Sui Discusses Her Spring 2012 Show and Punk Rock Heritage." *Rolling Stone*, September 14. http://www.rollingstone.com/music/blogs/thread-count/exclusive-anna-sui-discusses-her-spring-2012-show-and-punk-rock-heritage-20110914#ixzz1f1dLoERA. Accessed December 4, 2011.

Ogle, Jennifer Paff, and Molly Eckman. 2002. "Dress-Related Responses to the Columbine Shootings: Other-Imposed, Self-Designed." *Family and Consumer Sciences Research Journal* 31(2): 154–94.

Pappalardo, Anthony. 2012. "The First Chain of Strength in Interview in 20 Years Is Mostly about the Clothes." *Vice*. http://www.vice.com/read/the-first-chain-of-strength-interview-in-20-years-is-mostly-about-clothes. Accessed December 21, 2012.

Patterson, Elizabeth Gummere. 2007. "Say Something Outrageous: Punk Fashion, Capitalism and a New Future for the Avant-Garde." PhD diss., University of Colorado.

Peluchette, Joy, Katherine Karl, and Kathleen Rust. 2006. "Dressing to Impress: Beliefs and Attitudes Regarding Workplace Attire." *Journal of Business and Psychology* 21: 45–63.

Polhemus, Ted. 1994. *Street Style: From Sidewalk to Catwalk*. New York: Thames and Hudson.

Polhemus, Ted. 1996. *Style Surfing: What to Wear in the 3rd Millennium*. London: Thames and Hudson.

Polhemus, Ted. 2010. *Street Style: From Sidewalk to Catwalk*. 2nd ed. London: PYMCA.

Railla, Jean. 2007. "The Punk of Craft." *Craft* 1: 10.

Ramlijak, Suzanne. 2004. "Intimate Matter." In *Objects and Meaning: New Perspectives on Art and Craft*, ed. M. Anna Fariello and Paula Owen, 186–95. Oxford: Scarecrow Press.

Rannels, Melissa, Melissa Alvarado, and Hope Meng. 2006. *Sew Subversive: Down and Dirty for the Fabulous Fashionista*. Newtown, CT: Taunton Press.

Reynolds, Simon. 2011. *Retromania: Pop Culture's Addiction to Its Own Past*. London: Faber and Faber.

Roach, Mary Ellen, and Joanne Bubolz Eicher. 1965. *Dress Adornment and Social Order*. New York: John Wiley & Sons.

Roach-Higgins, Mary Ellen, and Joanne B. Eicher. 1992. "Dress and Identity." *Clothing and Textiles Research Journal* 10(4): 1–7.

Roeck, John, and Sherri Schottlaender. 1999. "Timeline." In *Forming: The Early Days of L.A. Punk*, ed. Track 16 Gallery, 46–71. Santa Monica, CA: Smart Art Press.

Rogers, Everett. 2003. *Diffusion of Innovations*. 5th ed. New York: Free Press.

Rombes, Nicholas. 2005. *The Ramones' Ramones (33 1/3)*. New York: Continuum.

Savage, Jon. 1991. *England's Dreaming: Anarchy, Sex Pistols, Punk Rock, and Beyond*. New York: St. Martin's Griffin.

Schmitt, Kaci. 2011. "Exploring Dress and Behavior of the Emo Subculture." PhD diss., Kennesaw State University.

"School Officials Tell another Wylie Student to Dye Her Hair." 2008. *NBC 5i News*, January 31. http://www.nbc5i.com/education/15181593/detail.html. Accessed February 15, 2008.

Schwartz, Barry. 2003. *The Paradox of Choice: Why More Is Less*. New York: Ecco.

Simmel, Georg. 1904. "Fashion." *International Quarterly* 10: 130–55.

Sklar, Monica. 2010. "Aesthetic Expressions: Punk Dress in the Workplace." PhD diss., University of Minnesota.

Sklar, Monica, and Marilyn Delong. 2012. "Punk Dress in the Workplace: Expression and Accommodation." *Clothing and Textiles Research Journal* 30(4): 285–99.

Sklar, Monica, and Lauren Michel. 2012. "The Punk Palette: Subversion through Color." In *Color and Design*, ed. Marilyn DeLong and Barbara Martinson, 150–6. London: Berg.

Slinkard, Petra. 2006. "Dreadlocks in Babylon: Motivations and Techniques for Wearing Dreadlocked Hair in Southern Indiana." Master's thesis, Indiana University.

Sparke, Penny. 2004. *Introduction to Design and Culture: 1900 to the Present*. 2nd ed. London: Routledge.

Spitz, Marc. 2011. "Generation X in a Time Capsule." *New York Times*, September 23. http://www.nytimes.com/2011/09/25/movies/homevideo/sonic-youth-film -1991-the-year-punk-broke-on-dvd.html?_r=0. Accessed January 17, 2013.

Sproles, George. 1974. "Fashion Theory: A Conceptual Framework." *Advances in Consumer Research* 1: 463–72.

Sproles, George. 1979. *Fashion: Consumer Behavior toward Dress*. Minneapolis, MN: Burgess.

Stoller, Debbie. 2003. *Stitch 'N Bitch: The Knitters' Handbook*. New York: Workman.

Stolper, Paul, and Andrew Wilson. 2004. *No Future: SEX, Seditionaries, and the Sex Pistols*. London: The Hospital.

Stone, Gregory, 1962. "Appearance and the Self." In *Human Behavior and the Social Processes: An Interactionist Approach*, ed. Arnold Marshall Rose, 86–116. New York: Houghton Mifflin.

Stryker, Sheldon. 1980. *Symbolic Interaction: A Social Structural Version*. Menlo Park, NJ: Benjamin Cummings.

Stryker, Sheldon, and Peter J. Burke. 2000. "The Past, Present, and Future of an Identity Theory." *Social Psychology Quarterly* 63(4): 284–97.

"Student Kicked Out of School For 'Distracting Hair.'" 2008. *WHAS 11 ABC News*, February 7. http://www.whas11.com/topstories/stories/whas_topstories_080206 _distractinghair.97b00981.html. Accessed February 15, 2008.

Sturken, Marita, and Lisa Cartwright. 2001. *Practices of Looking: An Introduction to Visual Culture*. Oxford: Oxford University Press.

Sweet, Derek. 2005. "More than Goth: The Rhetorical Reclamation of the Subcultural Self." *Popular Communication* 3(4): 239–64.

Sweetman, Paul. 1999. "Anchoring the (Postmodern) Self? Body Modification, Fashion, and Identity." *Body & Society* 5(1): 51–76.

Szatmary, David. 1996. *A Time to Rock: A Social History of Rock 'N' Roll*. New York: Schirmer Books.

Traber, Daniel S. 2008. "Locating the Punk Preppy (A Speculative Theory)." *The Journal of Popular Culture* 41(3): 488–508.

"T Screen Test Films: Lynn Hirschberg talks to Vivienne Westwood, Season 2, Episode 4." 2009. *The New York Times Style Magazine*. YouTube. http://www. YouTube.com/watch?v = qvj83Pr723Y. Accessed October 1, 2012.

Van Ham, Lane. 2009. "Reading Early Punk as Secularized Sacred Clowning." *Journal of Popular Culture* 42(2): 318–38.

Veblen, Thorstein. 1899. *The Theory of the Leisure Class: An Economic Study of Institutions*. New York: Macmillan.

Walker Art Center. 2007. "Elements and Principles of Today's Art." http://schools. walkerart.org:8083/arttoday/index.wac?id=2135. Accessed December 28, 2007.

Winge, Theresa. 2012. *Body Style*. London: Berg.

Wood, Robert T. 2003. "The Straight edge Youth Sub-Culture: Observations on the Complexity of a Sub-Cultural Identity." *Journal of Youth Studies* 6(1): 33–52.

Woodcock, Victoria. 2006. "Introduction." In *Making Stuff: An Alternative Craft Book*, ed. Ziggy Hanaor, 6–13. London: Black Dog.

Yeebo, Yepoka. 2012. "Inside The Last Surviving Punk Rock Boutique in New York City." *Business Insider*, February 12. http://www.businessinsider.com/inside -the-last-surviving-punk-rock-boutique-in-new-york-2012–2?op=1. Accessed August 21, 2012.

Guide to Further Reading

Subculture History and Analysis Including Discussions of Style

Bennett, A. 1999. "Subcultures or Neo-tribes? Rethinking the Relationship between Youth, Style and Musical Taste." *Sociology* 33(3): 599–617.

Featherstone, M. 1999. "Body Modification: An Introduction." *Body & Society* 5(2/3): 1–13.

Gelder, K., and S. Thornton. 1997. *The Subcultures Reader.* London: Routledge.

Hebdige, D. 1979. *Subculture: The Meaning of Style.* London: Routledge.

Holland, S. 2004. *Alternative Femininities: Body, Age, and Identity.* Oxford: Berg.

Muggleton, D. 2002. *Inside Subculture: The Postmodern Meaning of Style.* Oxford: Berg.

Muggleton, D., and R. Weinzierl. 2004. *The Post-subcultures Reader.* Oxford: Berg.

Steele, V. 1997. "Anti-fashion: The 1970s." *Fashion Theory* 1(3): 279–95.

Winge, T. 2012. *Body Style.* London: Berg.

Punk History (Some of the Discussion of Punk Style)

Anderson, M., and M. Jenkins. 2009. *Dance of Days: Two Decades of Punk in the Nation's Capital.* New York: Akashic Books.

Blush, S. 2001. *American Hardcore: A Tribal History.* Los Angeles: Feral House.

Leblanc, L. 1999. *Pretty in Punk: Girl's Gender Resistance in a Boy's Subculture.* New Brunswick, NJ: Rutgers University Press.

Marcus, G. 1990. *Lipstick Traces: A Secret History of the Twentieth Century.* Cambridge, MA: Harvard University Press.

Marcus, S. 2010. *Girls to the Front: The True Story of the Riot Grrrl Revolution.* New York: Harper Perennial.

McNeil, L., and G. McCain. 1996. *Please Kill Me: An Uncensored Oral History of Punk.* New York: Grove Press.

Moore, T., and B. Corley. 2008. *No Wave: Post-punk. Underground. New York. 1976–1980.* New York: Abrams Image.

Peterson, B. 2009. *Burning Fight: The Nineties Hardcore Revolution in Ethics, Politics, Spirit, and Sound.* Huntington Beach, CA: Revelation Records.

Savage, J. 1991. *England's Dreaming: Anarchy, the Sex Pistols, Punk Rock, and Beyond.* New York: St. Martin's Griffin.

Sinker, D. 2001. *We Owe You Nothing, Punk Planet: The Collected Interviews.* New York: Akashic Books.

Track 16 Gallery, eds. 1999. *Forming: The Early Days of L.A. Punk.* Santa Monica, CA: Smart Art Press.

Texts with Strong Emphasis on Punk Style

Bolton, A. 2013. *Punk: Chaos to Couture.* New York: Metropolitan Museum of Art.

Duffty, K., and P. Gorman. 2009. *Rebel Rebel: Anti-Style.* New York: Universe.

Levine, H., and S. Stumpf. 1983. "Statements of Fear through Cultural Symbols: Punk Rock as a Reflective Subculture." *Youth & Society* 14(4): 417–35.

Polhemus, T. 2010. *Street Style.* 2nd ed. London: PYMCA.

Sklar, M., and M. Delong. 2012. "Punk Dress in the Workplace: Expression and Accommodation." *Clothing and Textiles Research Journal* 30(4): 285–99.

Sklar, M., and L. Michel. 2012. "The Punk Palette: Subversion through Color." In *Color and Design*, ed. Marilyn DeLong and Barbara Martinson, 150–6. London: Berg.

Stolper, P., and A. Wilson. 2004. *No Future: SEX, Seditionaries, and the Sex Pistols.* London: The Hospital.

Wilcox, C. 2005. *Vivienne Westwood.* London: Victoria & Albert Museum.

Visual Culture Books Including Punk Style

Chernikowski, S., R. Bayley, and G. Dubose. 2000. *Blank Generation Revisited: The Early Days of Punk Rock.* New York: Schirmer Trade Books.

Colgrave, S., and C. Sullivan. 2001. *Punk: The Definitive Record of a Revolution.* New York: Thunder's Mouth Press.

Friedman, G., and C. R. Stecyk III. 1994. *Fuck You Heroes: Glen E. Friedman Photographs, 1976–1991.* Los Angeles: Burning Flags Press.

Jocoy, J., T. Moore, and E. Cervenka. 2002. *We're Desperate: The Punk Rock Photography of Jim Jocoy, SF/LA 1978–1980.* New York: PowerHouse Books.

Nedorostek, N., and A. Pappalardo. 2008. *Radio Silence: A Selected Visual History of American Hardcore Music.* New York: MTV Press.

Piper, C., G. Maryansky, and D. Brownwell. 1997. *The Unheard Music: Photographs, 1991–1997.* Denver, CO: P. A. Kane.

Index